The Democratization of Albania

Previous Publications

Theodore Kaltsounis, *Teaching Social Studies in the Elementary School* (1969).

Theodore Kaltsounis (with Celia Stendler Lavatelli and Walter J. Moore), *Elementary School Curriculum* (1972).

Theodore Kaltsounis, *Teaching Social Studies in the Elementary School: The Basics for Citizenship*, First and Second Editions (1979 and 1987).

Theodore Kaltsounis, *The World and Its People: States and Regions*, First and Second Editions (1982 and 1986).

Theodore Kaltsounis, *Geography of States and Regions* (1988).

The Democratization of Albania

Democracy from Within

Theodore Kaltsounis

palgrave
macmillan

THE DEMOCRATIZATION OF ALBANIA

First published in 2010 by
PALGRAVE MACMILLAN®
in the United States—a division of St. Martin's Press LLC,
175 Fifth Avenue, New York, NY 10010.

Where this book is distributed in the UK, Europe and the rest of the world, this is by Palgrave Macmillan, a division of Macmillan Publishers Limited, registered in England, company number 785998, of Houndmills, Basingstoke, Hampshire RG21 6XS.

Palgrave Macmillan is the global academic imprint of the above companies and has companies and representatives throughout the world.

Palgrave® and Macmillan® are registered trademarks in the United States, the United Kingdom, Europe and other countries.

ISBN: 978–0–230–10458–7

Library of Congress Cataloging-in-Publication Data

Kaltsounis, Theodore.
The democratization of Albania / Theodore Kaltsounis.
p. cm.
ISBN 978–0–230–10458–7 (alk. paper)
1. Democracy—Albania. 2. Democratization—Albania. 3. Albania—Politics and government. I. Title.

JN9689.A15K35 2009
320.94965—dc22 2009052012

A catalogue record of the book is available from the British Library.

Design by Newgen Imaging Systems (P) Ltd., Chennai, India.

First edition: August 2010

This book is dedicated
to my grandchildren
Christina
Ariana
Nicholas
Theodore
Andrew
Alexander
May they grow to become strong democracy builders.

Contents

Foreword

Theodore Kaltsounis has written a timely, important, and inspiring book. In a time when so many hopes for democracy around the world have been dashed, *The Democratization of Albania: Democracy from Within*, will raise the spirits of democracy activists everywhere.

Kaltsounis presents the story of the gradual democratic transformation of post-communist Albania—long one of the poorest countries in Europe, which suffered for decades under a particularly brutal Leninist dictatorship. This case study turns out to have multiple lessons for everyone interested in democratic reform.

First, Kaltsounis shows the profound impact of civic education on democratic participation, particularly among the young. In a period when social scientists have focused on the design of formal constitutions and electoral institutions as determinants of democracy, rather than longer-term changes in political culture, Kaltsounis's emphasis on education is a refreshing and welcome corrective.

Second, notwithstanding its subtitle, *Democracy from Within* also helps us understand much more clearly just what Western policymakers can do to support democracy "from without." Specifically, by targeting external grant funds to support principled teachers who support civic education in schools and universities in multiple regions over an extended period—instead of simply providing short-term aid to savvy operatives in the capital city, as so many failed efforts at democratization assistance have done in the past—Western donors can provide a crucial sense of security to key individuals within otherwise isolated democratic activist networks.

Third, Kaltsounis's book illustrates a remarkable personal journey on the part of the author, who left Albania as a child and who later became a noted scholar of civic education in the United

States. When the fall of communism in central and Eastern Europe allowed him to apply all the knowledge he has developed over his scholarly career, he eagerly embraced the challenge. The positive effect of Kaltsounis's two decades work in Albania thus clearly shows that the fate of democracy depends not only on favorable geography or socioeconomic factors—but also on the actions of committed individuals such as the author himself.

Stephen E. Hanson
Herbert J. Ellison Professor of Political Science and
Vice Provost for Global Affairs
University of Washington, Seattle

Acknowledgments

There are two groups of people that made this book possible: those in Albania who stood by me and contributed immensely in building the extensive democratization network in that country; and those closer to home who with their inspiration, support, and expertise helped make the project and this book possible.

I am grateful to the Albanian educators, including those in the universities, who opened their hearts and minds and accepted me and my proposals. The same is true of the country's authorities, and my leadership team of Albanian scholars, especially Dr. Marjana Sinani and Dr. Milika Dhamo, whose overwhelming commitment to the project is exemplary. Whatever has been achieved, it is also their achievement. It was their contributions—coming from within the country—that allowed the project to succeed. I will never forget that the spark for the project came out of discussions with Dr. John Louton, the then cultural officer of the American Embassy in Tirana. I am also grateful to the U.S. Department of State for funding the project, but more importantly, for its personnel's trust in me.

The book is a reflection of the successes we experienced in Albania, but neither the project nor the book would have been possible without the support and contributions of my colleagues at the University of Washington and that of my family and friends. Especially, I am most appreciative for the advice I received from my good friend and colleague Professor Norris Haring during the development of the project. His support was continuous and significant. Similarly, the book might have not happened without the encouragement of Professor Stephen E. Hanson, a distinguished colleague in the Department of Political Science. He saw the potential of the project and insisted that I write the book. His advice in the development of the manuscript was valuable.

Finally, my appreciation goes to my family and friends for standing by me, especially my wife, Maria, who for so many years endured my lengthy absences. She also read and advised me on the various phases of the manuscript. My friends Chris and Constance Gagas, as well as Bill Mallis, did the same. Last, but not least, my gratitude goes to my son Andreas and his wife Sarah, who took time from their busy schedules to provide me with their professional editorial advice and assistance.

Introduction

This book, *The Democratization of Albania: Democracy from Within,* deals mainly with democracy—its basic understanding, what it means to people in general, and the role of ordinary citizens in achieving and advancing a democratic way of life. It is appropriate, therefore, to start the book with a definition and a very brief historical sketch of democracy.

The contemporary definition of an established democracy usually combines the election of government leaders by universal suffrage and a number of elements rooted in the liberal movements of the seventeenth and eighteenth centuries, including, as Marc Plattner pointed out, "constitutional and limited government, the rule of law, and the protection of human rights."[1]

It is important to also note, especially as pertains to the project presented in this book, the suggestion by John Dewey that "democracy is more than a form of government; it is primarily a mode of associated living of conjoint communicated experience."[2] Dewey goes on to argue that the actions of an individual within the context of the community do affect and are affected by the actions of others, a reality that tends to generate tensions among people. Such tensions require dialogue, and a resolution that is consistent with the common good. If democracy is to function properly, self-interest needs to be restrained at times so that the good of the community can be served.

The origin of the word *democracy* is Greek and its literal translation to English is rule by the people. It was from this perspective that President Barack Obama of the United States recently defined democracy as he addressed Muslims around the world from Cairo. He argued that "all people yearn for certain things: the ability to speak your mind and have a say in how you are governed, confidence in the rule of law and the equal administration of justice, government that is transparent and doesn't steal from the people, the freedom to live as you choose." President Obama then continued, "These are not just American values. They are human rights."[3]

Forms of democracy always existed in small tribes and villages throughout the ages, but the Greeks were the first to give birth, more than 2,500 years ago, to a sophisticated democratic system of governance in the context of the city-state. Unfortunately, Athenian democracy was lost before it had a chance to grow to maturity. As a result, the democratic spirit was suppressed for centuries, but it did not die. Barely resurfacing in 1215 with the declaration of the Magna Carta in England, and strengthened by the various natural rights movements of the European Enlightenment, it questioned the validity of despotic rule and stimulated a search for a better way of life—one that would allow people to participate in building their own future.

The people (*demos* in Greek) learned again to want to have a say in the determination of their destiny. They developed an inclination to want to move away from authoritarian rule, and to rule by themselves. They developed an aspiration for democracy, but what should be the nature of that democracy? This question led to a lengthy debate that resulted in a number of European monarchies to give up absolute rule, adopt constitutions, and introduce various democratic institutions. The debate created uneasiness among the working classes that led to revolutions and to more democratic reforms. These reforms expanded beyond Europe to the various European colonies.

The people in the British colonies of North America, especially, demonstrated such a high level of aspiration for self rule that they declared their independence from Great Britain in 1776. Soon after, they adopted a constitution calling for the establishment of a republic with a democratic form of government. These developments led to the emergence of more democracies and set the stage for three significant modern waves of democracy with worldwide implications. The waves of democracy will be briefly presented later in the book to provide a background for Albania's democratization movement. It will suffice at this point to mention that Albania did not turn toward democracy until the early 1990s—almost two decades after the beginning of the third wave of democracy and following the collapse of the Soviet Union and Albania's own communist totalitarian regime.

In more specific terms, this book is about a University of Washington (UW) project I had the privilege of directing in Albania that sought to build democracy from within through her own educational system. In a way, the book is also a personal story since I was born in Albania among the Greek minority and lived there during my first fifteen years. Soon after Albania became a communist dictatorship, my immediate family and I escaped into Greece during the night, an undertaking that put our lives at risk. Forty-six years later, I returned to Albania for the first time to visit my relatives whom I have not seen, or heard from, since we left. The project was conceived during this trip and the funds to support it came from the U.S. Department of State, first through the United States Information Agency (USIA) and later the Bureau of Educational and Cultural Affairs. The funding started in 1992 and ended in 2005.

The first chapter of the book provides a background on Albania, stressing the fact that the country had practically no experience with democracy. The circumstances under which the project was conceived are also described. The decision to approach democratization from within, and from the bottom up, is a crucial element in this chapter. The second chapter addresses the steps taken to ensure that the project would be accepted by the Albanian authorities and supported by educators in the field. It also describes how the project worked with a special committee of the Pedagogical Research Institute of Tirana to arrive at a civic education curriculum for grades one through ten that would be oriented toward democracy. The chapter closes with a description of how open and interactive teaching was introduced to Albanian educators for the first time.

Chapters 3 and 4 deal with the identification and preparation of the core leadership team of the UW project. Consistent with the principle of "democracy from within," all members of the leadership team came from Albania. The basic concepts of democracy and the process of democratization are presented in considerable detail. Also described in these chapters is the development of a basic instructional manual and teacher's guides that reflect the interactive approach to teaching democracy. The emphasis in the manual and teacher's guides goes beyond the understanding of concepts related to democracy and address the application of these concepts in everyday life. Knowledge as well as democratic principles and skills were included. We aimed for the learners not only to use their intellect to understand democracy, but also to develop a passion for a democratic system as well as skill in the democratic way of life.

The fifth and sixth chapters show how a national network was established throughout the country for the promotion of democracy. Close to three thousand teachers, representing every school district in the country, were selected and trained on how to promote democracy using the instructional materials developed and published by the project. The network was then expanded by bringing the various nongovernmental organizations (NGOs), as well as the relevant international organizations, to play a part working by themselves or in partnership with the teachers. The problem of coping with bureaucratic delays is also described in these chapters.

The involvement of the universities in the democratization process of the country is presented in chapter 7. Five universities from throughout the country were identified and enthusiastically agreed to play a role in the continuing education of civic education teachers. A Civic Education Center with its own space was established in each campus and was equipped with a library, a computer, and other relevant equipment and materials. Two professors and six teachers from the area of each university were trained to manage their center, advise teachers in their area, and organize workshops for them. In addition, each center designed and carried out democratization activities at the local level, involving the university, the schools, and the community. The involvement of the universities was a very rewarding phase of the project, and the most promising one for the future of democratization in Albania and beyond.

Chapter 8 is devoted to an independent summative evaluation of the project by three scholars—one from the United States, one from Norway, and one from Albania. The evaluators spent a week in Albania traveling to various sites, observing various democratization activities, and talking to numerous individuals who were involved with the project or participated in project-related activities. In particular, they visited all five of the civic education centers and witnessed the set-up and operation of each center. The evaluators prepared a report and submitted it to a national civic education conference, which was attended by the minister of education and science, a representative of the American Embassy, and approximately one hundred teachers/educators from school districts throughout the country.

The two final chapters of the book, nine and ten, were an afterthought—after the first version of the manuscript was drafted. Though those of us directly involved with the UW project took pride in its accomplishments, it did not take us long to realize that the overall effort of democratization in Albania, as well as elsewhere, was not moving forward at a satisfactory pace. This was disappointing and formed a cloud over the future of democratization in general. As a result, I was not satisfied with just describing what the UW project accomplished in Albania. A way had to be found that could build upon our achievements and accelerate the process of democratization; probably a new model or just a new approach consisting of a combination of features from various existing models. Such an element would add to the book a dynamic quality that could advance democracy at a faster pace.

It was with these thoughts in mind that I decided to add chapters 9 and 10. In preparation for these chapters, I surveyed the democratization literature with an emphasis on existing democratization models. I also visited Brussels during the summer of 2008 to discover what the European Union (EU) was doing to help Albania build her democratic institutions. In addition, I went to Albania to determine whether the relevant players, especially those representing governmental institutions, were focused on the task of building democracy.

Serving as the foundation for a new approach to democratization, chapter 9 briefly presents the three waves of democracy, and their reverses, and assesses the viability of the various existing democratization models. Their strengths and weaknesses are analyzed in order to determine which model, or combination of models, best fits the approach used in Albania by the UW project. The chapter closes with the realization that models used thus far have not been adequately effective; that a new approach is needed to move Albania, and other countries in similar situations, faster toward consolidation of democracy—a level characterized by significant liberal policies and practices.

The tenth and final chapter starts with an assessment of what is currently happening in Albania. It explores the signs of progress in the democratization of the country, especially now that Albania is a member of the North Atlantic Treaty Organization (NATO) and is formally considered for admission to the EU. The evidence suggests that progress was made. In fact, Albania demonstrated enough progress to be classified by Freedom House in 2009 among the group of countries that received the highest overall score in the category of partly-free countries.[4] Unfortunately, however, Albania was rated unacceptably low in such critical areas as national democratic governance, judicial framework and independence, and corruption.[5]

But the most important part of this chapter is the articulation of a new approach to democratization—a model that is promising to accelerate the process. The proposed model calls for *ordinary citizens to become equal partners in the democratization of their country along with the government and the democratization professionals from outside the country.* As the most recent literature points out, especially an article by Christian Welzel and Ronald Inglehart,[6] ordinary citizens are the only ones in a position to pressure their government to do what needs to be done to advance democracy. Outside professionals can advise but they cannot compel a government to act upon their recommendations.

To be effective, however, ordinary citizens must be empowered for their role through education that is focused on democracy. As explained in chapter 10, Albania is fortunate in this respect, because the empowerment of the citizens can be achieved by taking advantage of the democratization network already established by the UW project. Under the enthusiastic leadership of the five university-based civic education centers, this network is capable of accomplishing the task.

In the final section of chapter 10, I discuss the potential of the book in advancing democracy. My goal is that it will serve as a source of inspiration and as an instrument for instruction on the subject. That it will be useful to all types of democratization workers at any level, including civic education teachers, social studies teachers, and teachers in general. My goal is that this book will be appreciated by college and university professors, governmental officials, nongovernmental and not-for-profit civic organizations and groups, and more importantly, the ordinary citizens. It conveys the basics of democracy by presenting not only the necessary knowledge, but also the commitment and action required on the part of each individual. It should never be forgotten that the people are the foundation upon which democracy rests. The people are also the source from which democracy gains its power to expand and move forward toward consolidation.

1

The Burden of the Past and Dreaming Democracy

Making a Difficult Decision

It was my strong desire to return to Albania for a visit. I wanted to see the village where I was born and raised for the first fifteen years of my life. Some would call this nostalgia, but I find that term too abstract to really explain my reasons for wanting to go back. In reality, it was what I left behind, and the experiences I took with me, that pushed me to return. My home was a two-room corner of a large two-storey house built by my father's uncle during the early part of the last century with money he earned in Egypt. It was the Kaltsounis House, or the *Kaltsounatiko*, as the locals used to call it. The people lived upstairs and used the ground floor mainly for storage. The animals, a couple of horses and a donkey, also lived inside the ground floor during the winter. The goats lived outside in a shed built by the men. Our corner was not much of a home, but I loved it and wanted to see it, touch it, and walk in it again.

There were about six to ten of us children living in that big house at that time. We had a lot of fun together. When the school was in session, we would all walk there together. But the school was not always open. After Mussolini took control of Albania in 1939, we went to school only a few weeks at a time. This was especially true after the Nazis moved in to help the Italians, who had been defeated by the Greeks. Every time the Nazis fought with the communist underground forces—the *partisans*[1]—the school would close until things calmed down and the Nazis withdrew to their bases. When the school was off, we would do chores or play outdoors. My basic chore was to go to the forest and load my donkey with wood for the fireplace or the brick oven my mother used for baking. One of the games we played often was a sort of a ball game using a ball we made from rugs. We would roll the cloth into a ball and tie it all around with a string. Then, with one of us standing by a tall stone wall, the rest would line up and take turns hitting him with the ball. The boy by the wall would move back and forth along the wall trying to avoid being hit. When someone missed, he would stand by the wall, and so on. Other times, we would organize ourselves into two groups and play war imitating the Nazis and the partisans. But we had hard time finding anyone in our group wanting to play the role of a Nazi.

My village was off the highway by approximately five miles and was usually under the control of the communists. But every couple of months the Nazis would stage a sweeping operation through the village and push the partisans higher up in the mountains. It was frightening to see the Nazis coming toward the village. Fortunately, they had to walk, and this gave us enough time to take some of our belongings to the woods to hide them, just in case the village was burned. Every time we saw the Nazis coming, all of us would go into the house and peek through the windows to see what was happening. We occasionally heard shots as the Nazis slowly walked through the village. The partisans rarely stayed to fight and usually fled to the mountains. They preferred to sneak up on the enemy and attack them when they least expected it.

As soon as the Nazis left the village, we would go outside to welcome back the partisans. Occasionally, we learned that someone's house was burned to the ground or that someone was killed. I vividly recall one partisan killed by the Nazis before he was able to escape. He was buried quickly in a shallow grave, his right arm still extending from the ground. His fist was clenched tightly in the typical salutation form of the communist rebels. I have no idea who did this or why they did it. As we watched, an underground soldier grabbed the dead man's arm and pulled his body out of the grave. That sight will stay with me forever. For most of us, this was the first dead person we had seen that closely. We were curious of everything but also frightened. Experiences such as these have a way of tying one to a place, especially at a young age. This kind of life continued until the Nazis were defeated in 1944 and the underground forces established their communist regime.

Then there were the relatives. I had not seen my uncle since I escaped from Albania forty-six years earlier. My uncle used to work in the fields and take care of the horses. The donkey was my responsibility. Several times during the year, we would travel to another village near the river to grow corn and rice. I was thrilled when my uncle gave me my own patch to grow rice, but I was never able to harvest it.

As I vividly recall, it had just rained and I was in the fields checking my patch to make sure it was dry enough for harvest. All of a sudden, I looked up and saw one of my cousins on his horse galloping toward me. Making sure no one was listening, he quietly informed me that my father had just arrived and together with my uncle and two of my aunts decided that our immediate family should escape into Greece. The reason for doing this was compelling. My older brother had just escaped and the law called for the rest of my family to be sent to exile in Northern Albania. But the fate of my father, a priest in the Orthodox Church, was uncertain. He had every reason to believe that he would be executed. A friend of his, who was working for the government, had warned him that all they were looking for was a good excuse. Under these circumstances, we had to leave, even though the risk was great. Every time I see the movie *Sound of Music*, it reminds me of our escape. Though it was difficult, we made it through the rugged mountains and eventually saw better days. However, that was not the case with the relatives left behind. They suffered a lot, just because we left. My relatives were discriminated in many ways, and they were constantly under surveillance. I just wanted to go to the village, give them a hug, and tell them how sorry I was.

Yes, I had a strong desire to go back to Albania, but I was afraid to do it. The communist regime had always punished anyone trying to escape from the country with death. Although the death penalty for this particular offense had just been lifted, I was still afraid that I would be arrested. Mr. G. John Doces, a distinguished businessman in the Seattle area, and a close friend, encouraged me to go with him. He also hailed from Southern Albania but left the country before the communists took over. My case was different, I thought, because I escaped during the time the communists were in power. Besides, Mr. Doces had recently visited Albania as a guest of the government of that country to advise them on how to improve production in a number of enterprises controlled by the government. My friend G. John even offered to make arrangements for me with the Rector of the University of Tirana to give a lecture on democracy at the university.

Going with Mr. Doces was somewhat reassuring, but I was still concerned that I might run into problems. So I called the U.S. Department of State and asked for the Albanian desk. I was informed that an Embassy had already been established in Albania, but with limited personnel, and was situated in the only hotel in Tirana existing for foreigners. The old American Embassy building was given to the Italians during the communist regime. They were going to evacuate it, but they needed more time. When I asked if I would have any protection, I was given a phone number to call Dr. John Louton who had just been appointed as Cultural Director of the American Embassy in Tirana. Dr. Louton turned out to be an alumnus of the University of Washington, having earned his Ph. D. from the School of International Studies. He encouraged me to go and promised to pick me up at the airport and be with me most of the time. When I revealed to him that I was born in Southern Albania among the Greek minority and would like to visit my village, he was excited. He found this to be a great opportunity for him to travel around the country and get to know people. He would try, he said, to make arrangements to go with me to my village. Being with Mr. Doces and having the support of the American Embassy's Cultural Director, I decided to go to Albania. I got myself a ticket and with Mr. Doces and his wife Sophia we flew to Tirana on October 1991.

CONDITIONS IN ALBANIA AND THE PEOPLE'S DEMAND FOR CHANGE

Though I had an idea of what I would find in Albania, the conditions were far worse than anything I could have imagined. As we approached the airport, we could see the uncultivated and neglected fields. Sheep were grazing next to the airport very close to the runway. The roads to Tirana and the city streets were in disrepair and practically empty. We saw more horse-driven carts than cars. Dilapidated housing developments were lined up along the streets all over the city. A number of public buildings at the center appeared old and in poor condition. We were taken directly to the hotel designated for foreigners, the same hotel in which the American Embassy was situated. It was full of news reporters from all over the world and others exploring possibilities for business opportunities.

Across the street from the hotel was a park full of people who had left the countryside looking for a better life. Some put a shack together and started a coffee shop or some other type of small business. Some of them were holding various items in their hands trying to sell them to passers-by. Others, especially children, were following people around asking for help. Some were just roaming around looking lost. Closer to the street was an empty marble pedestal. We found out later that a bust of Stalin used to sit on top of that pedestal reminding everyone of the connections between Albanian communism and the ruthless dictator of the Soviet Union. A short distance from the hotel, at the end of the street, one could see the main building of the country's flagship university with its original name, *ENVER HOXHA UNIVERSITY*, still visible even though the sign was taken down. The students had pulled the mounted letters out of the stone wall a few months earlier during a demonstration. The university was now referred to as the University of Tirana. Other monuments were also taken down forcibly, including the ten-meter-high statue of Enver Hoxha in the main square.

It did not take us very long to realize that the country was in turmoil. The people were restless. They were cautious at the beginning but they soon demonstrated defiance and boldness. They would stop showing up for work and eventually the collective farms would collapse. The peasants would steal animals for food or for starting their own small herd. The factories were short of labor and unproductive. Food shortages were evident, especially in the cities. Water and electricity were available only a few hours per day. Unemployment went high and the young people were looking for a way to get out of the country. The best gift you could give any Albanian toward the end of 1991 was a visa to get out of the country. Though I was not able to notify my relatives that I was going to be in Albania, some of them found out somehow and two cousins showed up at the hotel. All they wanted was a visa to go to Greece. By the time I attempted to go to the Greek Embassy, I had eight passports in my hands, including one from the taxi driver who took me there. I could not believe how happy he was getting that visa.

How did Albania get to be this way? Why were the Albanian people left behind the rest of Europe, and much of the rest of the world, in the pursuit of progress and a decent way of life? One must look into Albania's history for the answer. It is historically well established that the Albanians lived in the Western Balkans for a long time. Though questioned by some scholars,[2] the Albanians claim that they are descendants of the ancient Illyrians, who lived along the entire Adriatic coast. When the Illyrians fell under the Romans, the Albanians were absorbed within the Roman Empire along with the other people of that area. When the Roman Empire was later divided into two parts, the Albanians fell under the influence of the Eastern Roman Empire. This empire evolved into the Byzantine Empire and lasted until 1453 AD when Constantinople fell to the Ottoman Turks. The Albanians faced the Turks almost one hundred years earlier, but they did not give up easily. The Albanians fought against the Turks for twenty-five years under the leadership of Gjorgj Kastrioti, their most famous historical war hero, known as Skanderbeg. His statue, unlike that of Hohxa, still stands in the central square of Tirana, and it is highly revered by the Albanian people.

In the end, the Albanians—like all Balkan people—gave up and became a part of the Ottoman Empire. In the nineteenth century, most of the Balkan people were liberated after being inspired by the nationalistic movement. The Albanians, however, remained under Turkish control. One reason for this was, probably, the conversion of most Albanians to Islam. During the mid-nineteenth century, they wanted to join the nationalistic movement and establish their own schools in the Albanian language. The Turks would not allow them, however, telling them that as Muslims they were considered to be Turks and should send their children to Turkish schools. It was not until November 28, 1912, that the Albanians declared their independence from the Ottoman Empire. In fact, my father was born an Ottoman citizen and was five years old when Albania declared its independence. Due to the Balkan wars, World War I, and objections from neighboring nations, Albania was not consolidated as a sovereign nation until the end of 1920.

Forming an effective government in Albania turned out to be a difficult task. As Elez Biberaj points out, "[T]he semi-feudal Albanian society was characterized by widespread authoritarian tendencies, and apparently there were strong sentiments for the selection of a strong leader in the mold of Skanderbeg."[3] Political parties were established in the early 1920s and a Western-style government was formed that lasted only for few months. In Biberaj's words, "the main political parties engaged in endless feuding, the parliament was ineffective, and the country was plagued by political instability."[4] Ahmet Zogu, a chieftain from Northern Albania, took advantage of the situation and in 1924 forced himself into power. Four years later, he declared himself King of the Albanians. He ruled until Mussolini annexed Albania to Italy in 1939.

The Greeks defeated the Italians late in 1940 as they attempted to advance through Greece. The Nazis came to the rescue of the Italians and occupied Albania as well as the rest of the Balkan Peninsula. The occupation led to the emergence of underground forces. These forces were divided into those leaning to the right and those leaning to the left. The former were moved mainly by nationalism, while the latter were tied to the ideology of the international communist movement and were influenced by the Soviet Union. Initially, however, the communists promoted nationalism and gained the support of the majority of the people. When the Nazis left in 1944, the communists were able to prevail in Albania and formed a government under the leadership of Hoxha.

If feudalism, self-centered interests, and squabbling between various political leaders prevented Albanians from pursuing their happiness, Hoxha made things worse. He became one of the harshest dictators of modern times and set the stage for the Albanian people to suffer. Hoxha's policies served only his personal ambitions and prevented the ordinary citizen from moving forward. He stayed in power for forty years by eliminating opposition, confiscating all property and means of production, and forcing people to work in factories and collective farms mainly for the benefit of the government. He isolated the country from the rest of the world and used propaganda and severe punishment, including the death penalty, to keep people away from any source that would inspire them to think or act against his will. Religion was totally eliminated, radio listening and television viewing were limited only to government controlled domestic programs, and no traveling or any other type of contact with the outside world was allowed. Even official dealings with other countries were very selective. If Hoxha did not agree with the policies of a particular country, he would have nothing to do with it. He was able to survive and implement all of his policies with the help of a dreaded secret police—the *Sigurimi*—that carried out his severe punishments.

Before Hoxha died in 1985, he had picked Ramiz Alia to succeed him. Alia and his supporters in the Albanian Party of Labor (APL) had no intention of changing the system. Even the opening of the Soviet Union and the drastic changes in Eastern Europe did not have any immediate effect on Albania. Initially, the Albanian leadership blamed the revisionist policies of the Soviet Union for what was happening in Eastern Europe. Other times they would attribute various movements to hooliganism and declared them irrelevant to Albania. They also appealed to the people's patriotism. Seeing that their approach was not working, Alia tried to relax restrictions and reduce severe punishments for minor offenses. Travel outside the country was allowed, the practice of religion was reinstated, and the number of offenses deserving the death penalty was drastically reduced from thirty-four to eleven.[5] Some economic reforms were also attempted. People in the countryside, for example, were provided with a small plot to cultivate whatever they could for their own needs. At the same time, the tied grip of the secret police over the people was breaking down. There was even a question as to whether the armed forces would act against the people. Even within the APL some members were raising questions about human rights, including the imprisonment of political opponents.

The people sensed the uneasiness on the part of the government. As a result, their determination to free themselves from the yoke of the fifty-year-long harsh dictatorship became a mission for them, especially among the young people. On July 2, 1990, thousands of young people moved inside a number of Western embassies and refused to leave. Soon after that, four young members of the Kaltsounis family made the headlines by daring to cross the mountains into Greece under the leadership of Koula Kaltsounis, a very gutsy young lady. Koula did it, she told me later, to honor her late grandmother, after whom she was named. Her grandmother had been branded an enemy of the communist system and suffered in many ways, including imprisonment. All four of these young people are now in the United States. Demonstrations started in almost every part of the country, including a large one in Tirana on December 13, 1990, in support of the Democratic Party.

As months went by and the Albanian authorities gave up control of their borders, more people escaped to Montenegro, Greece, and Italy. My mother who lived in the Greek border town of Igoumenitsa became a destination point for just about everyone even remotely connected with the Kaltsounis family. Seeing their condition, she fed them, clothed them, and tried to meet their other needs as best as she could. What they wanted most to take back home was a refrigerator. She bought five of them before she ran out of money. She then turned to us, her children in the United States, to step in and help in any way we could.

Realizing that they were losing control of the situation, Alia and his supporters tried to introduce more reforms, but they no longer had the trust of the people. It was obvious that their motivation was simply self-preservation, though some of the elite were probably true Marxists and did not wish to abandon their philosophical base. But the people were ready to move on. They finally found out how people lived in the surrounding countries, and they started dreaming for a better life. As elaborated on later, Alia fell under the pressure of this dream.

Conceiving the Proposal for the Project

The first five days we spent in Tirana were memorable. We talked to many people, and we learned a lot about life in Albania and the problems they face daily. Mr. Doces had quite a few relatives in the city, and we were able to hear their personal stories. I also assisted Dr. Louton in many ways. I gave a series of talks to recently organized groups of people who had been persecuted by the regime. I interviewed and wrote recommendations for a number of young people who had applied to go to the United States for studies under the Fulbright Program. Giving the prearranged lecture on democracy at the University of Tirana, however, was not easy. The rector with whom Mr. Doces had made the arrangement had been replaced, and the new rector kept postponing the event for no obvious reason. Finally, a group of professors, on their own, called the faculty to a lecture hall and sent a delegation to the hotel to pick me up.

The professors were very attentive and receptive to what I had to say. At the end of the presentation, however, a rather young member of the faculty questioned the emphasis I placed on the concept of the common good. They have been hearing about the common good for fifty years, he explained, and he was surprised to get the same advice from an American. In response, I told the audience about my visit earlier that day to the neighborhood where Hoxha and his elite lived. That neighborhood was completely sealed from the public and was just opened that day for the first time. Compared to the conditions around the city, the neighborhood of Hoxha was luxurious. Then, I pointed out the main difference between the common good they have been serving for almost fifty years and the common good about which I was talking. It was not difficult to convince them that they were serving the common good as it was defined by one man as opposed to the common good I was advancing, which is to be defined by the people in a democratic way.

It was finally Friday morning and on Saturday Mr. and Mrs. Doces and I were to travel to our respective villages. We went downstairs for breakfast. We took a table and waited over a cup of coffee for Dr. Louton and the Charge d' Affairs of the Embassy, Mr. Christopher Hill, to join us. As soon as they approached, they looked as if they have not slept all night. We found out that they indeed did not sleep at all trying to evacuate an injured Albanian American couple to an American base in Germany. The couple was pushed off the road as they were driving north toward their village. The incident attracted a lot of attention from the media because the man was broadcasting in the Albanian language for the Voice of America for more than twenty years. Even Berisha, the leader of the newly formed Democratic Party, made a public statement blaming the government for the accident. When I heard all that, I questioned myself aloud whether I should go to my village. Sensing my concern and disappointment, Dr. Louton offered to go with me.

We met the next morning and started a journey of approximately two hundred and fifty miles. The love of the Albanian people for Americans being obvious, Dr. Louton attached more than one American flag on the car. As we traveled, we soon realized that the roads were winding and torn in many places. They were the same roads the Italians had built before World War II. We had to go slow. As we were driving south, we noticed that in every turn of the road, the hills on both sides were full of rounded concrete structures with narrow openings on the side facing the road. There were many of them. As we reached the area where the Greek minority was concentrated, these structures could be seen everywhere. A narrow plane near the city of Gjirokastra was lined up with series of such structures, one after the other cutting across the width of the plane. They were military bunkers, we were told, built to protect Albania from an imagined land invasion by neighboring countries. We also noticed another interesting defense mechanism. Many yards and fields were enclosed with fences that were attached to the ground by concrete posts. Extending from the top of each post was a six-to-eight-inches-long metal arrow with a sharp end pointing toward the sky. This unique instrument was to protect Albania from the air forces of neighboring countries.

We also noticed numerous monuments along the roads we drove on and the various towns we stopped in or drove through them. They were dedicated to Hoxha and to individuals who fell in battles during the war. Some monuments would be just a marble column with a red star and some kind of a communist propaganda message. Just about all of them were somehow defiled or completely destroyed by the people. We could justify the wrath against these monuments, but we could not understand why the people had chopped down the trees and destroyed what appeared to have been beautiful agricultural establishments, including vineyards and greenhouses. The answer, though, was simple. The people had worked and suffered a lot in those establishments without much benefit to themselves. They were too frustrated to think straight and save the trees and the various establishments for themselves in the near future. In their strong desire for drastic change, they were determined to destroy anything that reminded them of the past.

We finally reached the village. We traveled the last five miles on a dirt road and the going was difficult. For some peculiar reason, I asked Dr. Louton to drive not to my house but directly to a small Byzantine monastery at the edge of the village near my house. I was trying, I guess, to make a statement. I wanted to convey the message to my relatives and friends in the village to go back to their roots. Because of its historical value, the monastery was not destroyed like all other places of worship. Though I was very pleased it was still standing, my heart was broken to see the poor condition it was in. All the icons were gone. The beautiful Byzantine frescos around the walls were deteriorated. The eyes of some of the saints were poked with some kind of a sharp instrument. Everything was taken away, damaged, or destroyed. The walls were cracked. I could not help but wonder: Why? Noticing a crude stand in one side of the sanctuary, I approached it. Someone had placed on it a simple copy of an icon with the image of St. Nickolas, the patron saint of the monastery. A modest beginning, I thought, of a new era. With tears in my eyes, I kissed the icon, turned toward Dr. Louton, who was quietly observing every one of my moves, and we slowly walked outside.

A number of people had arrived in the courtyard wondering who these two strangers were. Hoping someone would remember or had heard about my father, who served as one of the priests in the village, I introduced myself as the son of Father Haralampos Kaltsounis. That was enough to start an emotional encounter with people I knew when we were young and the younger people that I was meeting for the first time. All of a sudden, I recognized my uncle Stavros as he was arriving. I ran toward him, we embraced each other and I could feel his heart pounding fast. The first thing he asked me was whether I visited Yugoslavia in 1971. As soon as I responded in the affirmative, he went on to tell me that the secret police had surrounded the Kaltsounis house at that time and were asking whether he had any communication from me. I was told later that someone in the village was assigned to continuously follow my movements. We all walked to the house where my uncle killed a goat and prepared a feast. I was soon part of the family and Dr. Louton was the guest of honor. He was the highest official of a foreign country to ever visit the village. The fact that he was representing the American Government made him even more important. They were counting on America to lead them to a better future.

It was a great celebration. Dr. Louton and I said goodbye to everyone and left for the nearby city of Sarande where we stayed overnight. As soon as we reached the main road, we started reflecting on the week's experiences. We were convinced that Albania was surely moving toward a new direction. The people were fed up with the past, and they were ready for change. What could we do to help? It did not take us long to conclude that if Albanians were to succeed they must integrate with the rest of Europe as soon as possible. To achieve that goal, it was necessary for Albania to move in the direction of eventually becoming a member of the European Union (EU). It was logical and probably easy for Albania to do so since both of her neighbors, Italy to the west and Greece to the east, were already members. Europe would want that to happen, provided the Albanians worked hard to meet the criteria for admission. The most important of these criteria would be the development of democratic institutions, respect for human rights, and a free market economy. In other words, Albania would have to be completely transformed as a nation. The country would have to abandon authoritarian rule, respect the individual and his or her rights, allow people to freely express their will, have equal opportunity, and return property to the people.

As we recounted the sociopolitical developments during the last few months, we felt confident that the time was ripe for Albania to move in the direction of Europeanization and democratization. Though the communists had won the national elections on March 31, 1991, the demonstrations continued and the labor unions staged a strike, openly demanding their independence. In view of the pressures, the new government installed under the leadership of Fatos Nano had resigned early in June. After a bitter debate among themselves, the members of APL had renounced Stalinism in July, rejected Marxism and Leninism, and changed the name of their party to the Albanian Socialist Party. Finally, President Alia resigned and a coalition government emerged with Ulli Bufi as prime minister. The parliament had resolved to have new general elections no later than June 1992 with the participation of multiple political parties. As these developments were rapidly taking place, the situation in the country was becoming desperate. The international community was requested and came to the rescue with assistance. At the same time, Albania was admitted as a full member to the Conference on Security and Cooperation in Europe.[6]

We arrived at the hotel, checked in, and each of us went directly to his room. Though it had been a long day, I was wide awake thinking about the day and the type of a specific project that could contribute toward the democratization of Albania. All of a sudden, I questioned myself as to whether I was the right person to undertake such a project. Yes, I did live in Albania during the first fifteen years of my life but my ethnicity and that of most of the people around me was Greek. As a matter of fact, I never learned the Albanian language. My mother tongue was Greek. I grew up with the dream of some day going to Greece for studies. When our family escaped and I was finally in Greece, I felt comfortable being with Greek people. I never had that feeling about the people from other countries. The Italians were bad, I thought, because they came with boats and cannons during the night and invaded our area when I was nine years old. Shortly after the invasion, they came through our village on their way to attack Greece. As a result, I was afraid of them and learned to dislike them. When the Nazis came later they were worse. I personally never had any bad experiences with the Albanians, but every time I went through a village where the people spoke Albanian, I was afraid of them just as much as I was afraid of the Italians or the Germans. I was even more afraid if I knew the people in a particular village were Muslim. The war and national bickering made me that way.

Fortunately, I moved away when I was young and changed my thinking and my view of the world. The breakthrough happened when I had just completed the equivalent of a high school education in a Greek school that was founded and supported by the archbishop of Athens and All of Greece. At the request of the archbishop, an American came to our school to select a student for participation in an international work camp in our area. The camp was sponsored by the World Council of Churches. The objective of the project was to build an irrigation system for a nearby village. The American showed us slides with scenes from a previous camp, and I saw students from America, Italy, England, Bulgaria, Germany, and other countries living and working together. Following the presentation, he asked to meet with those of us interested in submitting an application. None of us were interested in applying because we did not want to live and work with people from countries we learned to dislike during the war. This was an embarrassment for the director of the school, who called me in his office to tell me that we could not disappoint the archbishop. He recommended that I apply for the camp. In reality that was not just a recommendation. I had no choice but to comply, but I was counting on not being selected since a foreign language was desirable and I did not speak any of them. A few days later, I was sad to find out that I was selected for the camp.

The American came back in a few days to take me to meet the first group of participants, who had just arrived from other countries. I climbed on his jeep and off we went. When we approached the place where the students stayed overnight, they were sitting on the stairways by the entry of the building reading or writing postcards. As soon as the American told them who I was, they all stood and came to greet me. What a warm welcome from a group of strangers! Based on my past experiences with people from other countries, I never expected it. I was overwhelmed and for the first time I was glad I applied to go to the camp. I could not wait to go back to my school and tell the director what happened and that I was looking forward to participating in the camp. That experience was the beginning of my journey to the world. Today, I am where I am, and who I am, because of that work camp.

The experience just described provided me with the opportunity to learn to respect people regardless of their ethnic origin, language, religion, or the country in which they live. I learned that the world is too small to continue bickering and fighting with each other. I discovered broader and nobler principles that helped me rise above the narrow vision of nationalism—just my country and my people kind of attitude. Whatever the differences, we all need to work together in peaceful ways so that all of us can reach our potential and achieve our dreams. With these thoughts in mind, I decided that I would work in Albania to assist in any way I could to help bring democracy to that country. I knew I would have to convince the Albanians about this, but I was confident that I could do it. The thought also occurred to me that I might risk being considered a traitor by some in the Greek minority, but I quickly dismissed that thought. I was convinced that what I was about to do was resting on higher principles and values. I believed that spreading democracy in any part of the Balkans would benefit everyone living in that part of the world. They all had to accept each other and live together peacefully in a free and prosperous Europe.

DEVELOPING DEMOCRACY FROM WITHIN

Dr. Louton and I had breakfast in the morning and started our long journey back to Tirana. We soon picked up our discussion from where we left it the previous day. I could not help but share with him what went through my mind during the last evening. He demonstrated great interest in my dilemmas but he saw no problem. We resolved to concentrate on developing and undertaking a proposal for a democratization project in Albania. I was to develop the proposal to go through the University of Washington, and he would explore funding possibilities, including the United States Information Agency and the U.S. Department of State. Since we had plenty of time before reaching Tirana, we embarked on a discussion that helped me later to develop the basic guidelines that would characterize and shape the project. They were as follows:

- The basic concepts of democracy and those of the democratic process should be clearly identified. Moreover, the concepts relating to the social aspects of democracy should be just as important as those relating to the political aspects of democracy. Learning how to get along with each other is just as important as learning the process of how a bill becomes a law.
- In a country where the older generation grew up under the influence of a totalitarian regime, the teaching of democracy should start with the young people—the future generation.
- Since Albania had little experience with democracy, the project should be comprehensive and cover the entire country. The usual practice of simply demonstrating open teaching, for example, or any other aspect of democratic citizenship education to a few teachers and students would not be adequate. A nationwide network would be needed.
- Along with advancing an understanding of the conceptual framework of democracy, the school curriculum should be designed to develop commitment to the basic principles and values of democracy and the ability to practice these principles and values in daily life. In other words, the curriculum would need to develop everyone into a democrat for democracy to work. The strength and longevity of a democracy rest more on the people than on its leaders.
- Open and interactive teaching should be applied in teaching democracy. We determined that was the only way to develop committed and skillful democrats. Children and youth would learn to practice democracy in the arenas of the school, neighborhood, and the larger community.

- The approval and support of the establishment, especially the government, would be important for the success of a democratization project.
- Most importantly, democracy should be developed from within. Democracy cannot be transplanted or imposed, especially by force, from the outside. The people of a particular country develop democracy.

2

Building Relationships and Exploring Curriculum

Contemplating the Project Scope and the Beginning

After returning to the United States, it was time for me to develop a proposal that would reflect the guidelines Dr. Louton and I discussed. That meant the project had to be broad and comprehensive involving the entire country of Albania. My College at the University of Washington was supportive and I knew I could do it. My passion for democracy was strong. I had experienced life in the American democracy after living in countries where democracy did not exist or was plagued by nondemocratic ways. That experience enabled me to see the difference and develop strong appreciation for the democratic systems. Though America is not perfect, you can trust institutions to address the concerns and aspirations of its citizens. In America you do not need to know someone to be served by the system. Social mobility is possible and easier than it is in most other parts of the world. You are not forever locked into any particular social context. You can dream for a better life and achieve it through hard work. In sum, meritocracy is a stronger value in America than in the countries in which I grew up. I came to America with ten dollars in my pocket and was able to pursue studies to the maximum. When I decided to stay, my credentials made it possible for me to get a position and advance regardless of my accent or the fact that I grew up somewhere else. What counts is not who you are or where you came from, but rather what you can do.

Inspired by the realizations just expressed, it did not take me long after arriving in America to switch from an observant visitor to an active participant in the democratic process. As a professor of social studies education, I prepared teachers to teach social studies in elementary and secondary schools. When I saw that an antiquated social studies curriculum was ignoring the deliberate teaching of democracy, I did not hesitate to raise my voice. In 1971, I wrote a major article for *Instructor* magazine with the title "Swing toward Decision Making."[1] The emphasis in that article was the development of democratic skills. When I was elected vice president of the National Council for the Social Studies (NCSS) in1980, I was invited to give the keynote address at the annual meeting of the Texas Council for the Social Studies. The topic I selected was "Don't take democracy for granted." After pointing out that democracy is a state of civilization, I warned the audience that it can deteriorate if not deliberately taught. Then, to demonstrate how difficult life can be without democracy, I gave the teachers one example after the other from my own personal experiences in communist Albania and the 1967–1974 dictatorship in Greece. It was the first time in my career that I received an enthusiastic standing ovation from an audience of approximately 800 people.

Since that experience in Texas, I decided to promote democracy as the main focus of social studies education. The following year, democracy was the central theme of my travels around the country as president of NCSS. I developed and taught a new graduate course on teaching democracy that was received very well by teachers. Some of them made a name for themselves because of the emphasis they placed on democracy in their teaching. The students of these teachers were very excited as they were asked to implement democratic principles and skills in their everyday lives within the school and the community. As a social studies textbook author with a major textbook company during the 1980s and 1990s, I made sure democratic principles and skills were not left out of the curriculum. The Korean Educational Development Institute invited me to Korea to work with them on democratic citizenship education. I also traveled to Taiwan and other countries, including Greece, under the auspices of the United States Information Agency (USIA) to promote democratic citizenship education. Lastly, I published an article in *Theory and Research in Social Education* challenging educators to make democracy the foundation of the social studies curriculum in schools.[2]

Yes, my passion for democracy, my experience in learning about and teaching democracy, along with the guidelines Dr. Louton and I worked on, gave me the courage to believe that I could develop a proposal that could make a difference in Albania. In accordance with the guidelines, the democratization of Albania would start with the younger generation through the involvement of the entire educational system. The educational establishment of the country would provide the extensive network needed to spread democracy to every corner of Albania. With the proper plan, the parents and most other adults in the various communities would also be impacted. For a number of reasons, however, it was difficult to develop these guidelines into an overall plan. We had no idea what it would cost to undertake such an extensive project or whether we could raise the required funds. In addition, in view of our strong belief that democratization would need to come form within, we were not in a position to define the steps of the project without the participation of the Albanians. And of all the Albanians, we needed the support of the Albanian Ministry of Education and its institutions. Only with their approval and assistance could we proceed with the selection of a small leadership team to work with us and eventually assume responsibility for the activities of the project within Albania. This team would also be vitally instrumental in advancing the overall project toward new horizons.

To obtain the Ministry of Education's support we decided to initially develop a short-range proposal for a number of activities with the following goals: (1) convince the higher echelon of the Albanian Ministry of Education to allow the undertaking of the project; (2) develop trust between the Ministry of Education, the University of Washington, and me personally as the director of the project; (3) organize a series of workshops in various parts of the country to demonstrate open and interactive teaching; (4) explore and familiarize ourselves with the Albanian school curriculum, especially the social studies component of it; and (5) determine the way in which to integrate the teaching of democracy in the curriculum.

This initial proposal was developed during the early part of 1992. A number of individuals came to my assistance as I was developing it. I am especially indebted to my friend and colleague Professor Norris Haring, a renowned scholar in the field of Special

Education. He listened to me over numerous cups of coffee and gave me valuable advice, especially on the overall plans for the project and on budget matters. He even incorporated my project in the research unit of his academic area. The proposal was submitted to the USIA for funding and was approved during the summer of the same year.

Buying-in and Achieving Credibility

Following the proposal's approval, a direct request was made to the Albanian Minister of Education to send ten of the highest echelon of his Ministry to the University of Washington for three weeks. We also proposed that the visit take place toward the latter part of November 1992. The purpose of the visit was to provide opportunities for the visitors to learn about democracy. They would participate in seminars to hear about and discuss theoretical aspects of the system. They would also observe democracy in action in American communities. Especially, we wanted them to observe democratic ways to teach and educate teachers, to establish educational policy, and to develop school curriculum. The most important objective of the visit, however, was to get to know them and listen to their reactions to our plans for the project. In the process, we hoped that we would earn their trust. In other words, we were working hard toward achieving their commitment—buying in—to the project.

As we made final arrangements for the various activities, we faced the typical Balkan practice of no timely response from Albania to our requests. We had asked for a list with the names of the individuals selected for the trip, and we suggested the date for their arrival in Seattle. The proposed date was rapidly approaching and there was no response. Since Dr. Louton had left Albania for another post, I asked his replacement to intervene with the Ministry of Education. Someone in the Ministry indicated that they were working at it, but we continued to be on a waiting mode. Finally, I called the Ministry of Education directly and asked to speak with the minister. He assured me that the list will be on its way. Within a few days, we had the names of the officials and the date and time of their arrival. Included in the list were: The Director General of Secondary Education, the Director General of Elementary Education, the Inspector General of Secondary

Education, the Inspector General of Elementary Education, the Director of the Pedagogical Research and Development Institute of Tirana, a Professor of Education from the University of Tirana, another Professor of Education from the University of Elbasan, and a teacher. Another official from the Textbook Division of the Ministry Education was already in Seattle working with me under the Fulbright Program. He also joined the group and participated in all the discussions and other activities.

The time of arrival came and I went to the airport to pick up our distinguished guests with a university van big enough to accommodate the people and their luggage. As we waited for the luggage, I pulled aside the leader of the group, who spoke English, and informed him that the budget provided for each one of them $125.00 per day for lodging, food, and other personal expenses. Then, I explained to him that there were two options available to them: they could stay in a hotel where they would spend most of their daily allocation to pay for the room; or I could arrange for them to stay in a university dormitory and pay less than $20.00 per night. I did this because I became aware during my trip to Albania that the wages in that country were very low at that time. A typical worker was earning less than one dollar a day. The Ministry officials' salaries were quite a bit higher than that, but still very low compared to our standards. The gentleman quietly thanked me for understanding their situation and opted for the dormitories. Some even chose to team up as roommates to save additional dollars.

During the first few days of their visit, I walked around Seattle with my guests, attended a number of special seminars on democracy, and visited a number of schools to observe teaching. They especially enjoyed a class taught by Paula Frazer, a dynamic fifth-grade teacher who had taken my course on teaching about democracy. Paula was very passionate in teaching the democratic ways and principles. She was inspirational not only to her students but also to anyone visiting her class. When the class was over, we discussed Paula's teaching and it was obvious that they were impressed by the way she guided her students to openly discuss social issues relating to their classroom, the school, and the local community. I told my guests that it was my dream to work hard with them to create for Albania as many teachers like Paula as possible. One evening we attended the school-board meeting of a rather large school district. My guests saw how the board operated and, at the end, witnessed the parents and the public questioning the board on a number of issues.

One day we traveled to the capital of the State of Washington to visit the three branches of the government—the executive, the legislative, and the judicial. As we entered the office suite of the Secretary of State, the secretary himself happened to be right at the entrance. He welcomed us, and as soon as he discovered who my guests were, he invited everyone in his office. We had a delightful discussion and then walked to the Washington State Governor's office on the other side of the building. The governor was not there but his secretary took us inside his office and explained the symbolism of the various items displayed in it. All types of people were sitting in the outer room waiting for the governor. One of my guests sat next to a man in shorts and asked him why he wanted to see the governor. The man responded that his son was in some kind of a problem and he felt the governor could help. The guest turned then to me and asked where all the guards were. He was surprised to find out that there were not any of them around. Unfortunately, the situation had to change after the attacks of 9/11.[3]

Half way through the visit, the group traveled to Detroit to participate in the three-day annual meeting of NCSS. The membership of this organization consists of thousands of social studies teachers and university professors of social studies education from throughout the country. The purpose of this activity was to accomplish the following objectives: (1) expose our guests to deliberation of social studies curriculum issues and inform them on the process of curriculum development; (2) inform our guests on the philosophy and process of textbook development and distribution in the United States; (3) provide our guests with the opportunity to see the variety of new textbooks and other social studies instructional materials exhibited at the meeting; and (4) inform our guests on the multicultural aspects of American education, which is an important aspect of American education, and a requirement of the funding agency. In view of the fact that several of our guests could not speak English, the U.S. Department of State provided us with interpreters and a system of microphones for simultaneous translation.

At the conference, my guests made the significant discovery that neither the U.S. Government nor the state governments are involved in curriculum development. Instead, the specialists in social studies education deliberate the curriculum issues and arrive at recommendations. Because the debates take place at the annual meeting, teachers and other types of educators have the opportunity to also participate by reacting to the various proposals and recommendations. We planned in advance to make sure our guests attended an adequate number of sessions on curriculum issues. At the end of each session, we had a brief meeting among ourselves to deal with any questions that might have been generated by what was presented and discussed in the session.

As my guests learned, the information produced during the annual meeting ends up being published in various professional journals, mainly *Social Education, The Social Studies*, and *Theory and Research in Social Education*. Another important way in which the information is disseminated is through the various textbook publishing companies—all of them private. Each one of them sends their editors and other decision makers to the annual meeting to familiarize themselves with the latest developments and trends. At the same time, they try to identify the leaders among the scholars in social studies curriculum. These leading scholars are then invited by the companies to work with their editors to produce new textbooks or to revise the ones they already have in the market. The companies then sell the books throughout the country.

The approach to selling and buying textbooks varies from school district to school district and from state to state. In very few states, a committee evaluates the books of major competing companies and approves three to five companies from which the districts can choose. In most states, however, each school district evaluates the products of the various publishers and selects one for the schools in their district. There are also a few cases where each school chooses whatever publisher they feel better meets their objectives. I was fortunate to have worked with the Silver-Burdett company on a kindergarten-eighth grade series of textbooks that turned out to be the most dominant one during the 1980s and 1990s.

My Albanian guests enjoyed the sessions. Only once did one of them suggest that there was no need for them to attend any sessions on multicultural education. Albania, he argued, is a rather uniform society and multicultural education was not something in which to invest their time. Coming from a minority in Albania myself, I found that suggestion quite telling, but I decided not to react other than to say that it was a requirement from the funding agency. Contrary to my guest's suggestion, Elez Biberaj has noted that there are sizable minorities in Albania consisting of Greeks, Slavs, Vlachs, and Roma.[4] The part of the visit the Albanians enjoyed immensely was the exhibit of the textbooks and other instructional materials. Since I knew several of the authors and representatives of publishers, I introduced my guests to them and explained the reason for their visit. All the publishers were delighted to meet the group and they loaded each one of them with whatever appealed to them, free of charge. Little did the donors know that those books would later help shape the Albanian social studies curriculum.

Upon returning to Seattle, it was time for the Thanksgiving recess. All guests were invited by members of the university faculty to their home to have dinner with them and their families. Needles to say, our guests were overwhelmed with the demonstrated hospitality and made new friends. We also took time to go shopping but this endeavor turned out to be as difficult as it was interesting. Thanks to the dormitory arrangement and the availability of plenty fast-food establishments in the university district neighborhood, our guests saved some money for shopping. We started with the main department stores in the city. The Albanian visitors walked around and looked at merchandise, but they showed no interest in buying anything. They found the prices to be too high. One of them had heard of K-Mart as a store with reasonable prices, but they found that store, as well, too expensive for them. Then I thought of a friend of mine who owned a store with second-hand clothing. Not wanting to insult them, I was reluctant to take them to that store. Their leader, however, suggested that we should go. We drove there, and while they were looking around, I quietly explained to the owner who the visitors were and the problem they were facing with the high prices in the department stores. He offered to sell to them anything in the store at half price. Hearing that, they ran to the section where used suitcases were displayed for sale. They took them all and filled them with clothes. I warned them that they could not take more than two suitcases at the airplane, but they ignored the warning.

The end of the three weeks was approaching. The indications were that they had a pleasant and rewarding experience. They could not say enough to thank me for the opportunity to come to America. Knowing that I grew up in Southern Albania, they considered me to be one of them. In fact, when the president of the university welcomed them to his office one day, the leader of the group thanked the president and indicated how pleased they were to be in Seattle, especially, he added, under the aegis of Professor Kaltsounis who is an Albanian. I smiled and said nothing. All through the visit, I could not help but notice an interest on their part to know what I was claiming to be—Albanian, Greek, or American. I perceived that to be their typical Balkan nationalistic spirit at work.

The evening before their planned departure, I suggested to my wife that we visit the group at their dormitories. She made a cake, prepared a pot of coffee and we went to see them. We all gathered in a meeting room and after we had some cake and refilled our cup with coffee, I spoke a few words to them:

> You have been in Seattle for three weeks. I hope this experience made you a little bit less Albanian in your mentality and to some degree more internationally minded. Nationalism is dead or dying. If we are to move forward in this world and all of us are to live together in peace, we must learn how to get along with each other. Each one of us must learn to feel comfortable wherever we are. Take me, for example. I have the privilege of being claimed by three counties—Albania because I was born and lived in that country during the first fifteen years of my life; Greece because that is where the roots of my culture and religion are, Greek is my mother tongue, and that is where I went to high school and teachers college; and America, because that is where I received my higher education, developed my career, and created my family. I feel comfortable with all three of these countries. I worked hard in Greece to the point where I was included in Who's Who in Greece, I worked hard in America to the point where I was included in Who's Who in America, and now that Albania is open, I am willing to also work hard in that country and hope that some day I will be included in Who's Who in Albania.

The reaction to those brief comments was amazing. I felt that I was able to move the group beyond nationalism and effectively challenged them to reach higher and deal with concepts and ideals that transcend nationalism. I felt that both of us, them and I, put the past behind us and were ready to work together for the sake of democracy. They recognized the potential value of the project, and I established my credibility with them. It was a wonderful feeling for all of us as they left for their rooms to pack for the airport. I was convinced that my mission was accomplished. As far as the excessive number of suitcases is concerned, an airline supervisor empathized with the situation and loaded every one of them on the airplane.

EXPERIENCING OPEN AND INTERACTIVE TEACHING

Three months later I was back in Albania. Although it had been only three months since I met the Ministry officials, I felt upon my arrival in Tirana that I was seeing old friends that I had not seen for years. During the preparations for my trip, I was constantly in touch with them, especially with the English-speaking Director General of Secondary Education, Dr. Vili Minaroli. This true gentleman had served as the leader of the group while in Seattle. Since the situation in Albania was evolving very fast, I needed current information to prepare a budget for my trip. For example, I needed to know what a hotel room would cost per day. Since I did not speak Albanian, I also needed to know how much it would cost per day to hire an interpreter. How about the cost per day to rent a car and driver? More importantly, I needed appointments with various officials, including the minister of education, to explain the project, gain his support, and thus expand my network. I also wanted to meet with any committee or specialists working on curriculum development and the preparation of textbooks in social studies or any subject that might be related in some way to civic education. Dr. Minaroli went out of his way to assist with every one of the requests made to him.

The plans for the trip also included a series of workshops throughout the country with selected teachers and other types of educators. Earning the support of these educators, and thus expanding the network, was again the purpose of the workshops. Dr. Laura Wendling, now a professor of social studies education at California State University at San Marcos, came with me from Seattle to demonstrate open teaching and discuss it with the participants. Dr. Minaroli and the rest of our friends in the Ministry of Education organized the workshops in the cities of Shkodra, Tirana, Elbasan, Korca, and Gjirokastra. They also traveled with us to other cities located throughout the country from the far north to the far south. The two-hour workshops consisted of a demonstration of open and interactive teaching. As a matter of fact, the title of the proposal to the USIA for this segment of the project was "From Propaganda to Teaching." The last half of an hour was devoted to obtaining written suggestions from the participants on changes they would like to see in the country's educational system.

Before expanding on the workshops, it is important at this point to note the enthusiastic and warm welcome extended to us by our friends in the Ministry of Education. Several of them met us at the airport and made sure we were treated like dignitaries. We were driven to the hotel and early the next day they drove us to the Ministry of Education for a meeting with the minister. What a wonderful meeting! The minister was pleasant and listened carefully as the overall objectives of the project were presented to him. He expressed his appreciation for what we were trying to do and instructed those present from his staff to provide us whatever assistance we needed. As a matter of fact, he offered his car and driver to use while we were in Tirana. I was convinced that democratization would move forward in Albania under his leadership.

Returning to the workshops, one of their objectives was to demonstrate interactive teaching through the application of the inductive approach to learning. Interactive teaching implies that a particular concept is learned through verbal exchanges between the teacher and the students rather than by the teacher just lecturing to them about the concept. In other words, the teacher leads the students, induces them, to the understanding of a concept with questions, discussions, and occasional injections of appropriate information. Dr. Wendling used a number of concepts in demonstrating the process; for the purpose of this section, I will use the concept of democracy to show how she did it. The first question by the teacher would be to ask the students to suggest any characteristic of democracy that comes to mind. This will produce a rather long list of characteristics. The list is then displayed for examination. Elections and a government with three branches, for example, may be included in the list as characteristics of democracy, but the instructor would question whether these characteristics are critical. Are they among those which distinguish democracy from other systems? They are not because totalitarian regimes may also have elections, but not be free; or a government may have three branches but the judiciary is not independent of the other two, especially the executive. At the end of the discussion, the only characteristics to remain indisputable are human rights and sovereignty of the people.

Another objective of the workshops was a demonstration on how to deal with controversial issues. In a democracy, the people are often called upon to resolve such issues, but are they prepared for the task? Are they inclined and able to consider all sides of an issue? Are they equipped and strong enough to make compromises? Are they able to rise above narrow interests and address issues from the point of view of the common good? As Dr. Wendling demonstrated, students can start learning how to resolve issues by practicing on resolving their own classroom problems under the guidance of the teacher. If it is noisy in their classroom, for example, how can they improve the situation? What rules can they establish that are fair, and how should these rules be enforced? With such questions, the teacher serves as a leader in having the students resolve the noise problem, or any other problem, rather than the teacher imposing his/her authority. The approach proves to be more effective and provides for long-lasting learning. If they get into the habit of resolving their problems in a fair and considerate manner now, the chances are, they will do the same later on in their adult lives. Not involving the students in dealing with school conflicts now deprives them of the ability to deal with conflicts later. That will deprive society of valuable citizens.

The Albanian educators were sharp and pleasant to work with on an individual basis. Overall, they were receptive of the type of teaching we were demonstrating, and they were looking forward to changes. They were, however, showing a lack of proper demeanor in the context of a discussion. They were very attentive to Dr. Wendling, but when one of them was speaking in response to a question, the rest of them would resort to private discussions with the persons around them. Needles to say, this made it difficult to carry on a discussion. Dr. Wendling would call for their attention, but the behavior continued. Finally, I had to intervene by suggesting that if we paid attention to what everyone in the group was saying we could all learn from each other. It appeared that the only thing they were interested in doing was to grasp any opportunity they could to deliver a short speech. The situation started to improve when a couple engaged in a private discussion was politely asked to continue their discussion outside the meeting room. They finally realized that we meant business and adapted to the protocol of a good discussion.

An interesting episode in the most Northern city of Shkodra led us to realize that we had much to do to assist Albanians to understand democracy and its processes. It was time for lunch and the suggestion was made to go eat at a newly established private restaurant in town. Since the communist regime had not allowed private businesses, this was a new experience for the Albanians. As we approached the restaurant, the owner met us outside and pleaded with us not to go inside due to a fight in progress between two of his customers. One person from our group asked whether the police had been called. We were informed that two policemen were already inside dealing with the situation. Within minutes, the policemen emerged from inside the restaurant looking perplexed. They advised us not to enter the restaurant because the two men continued to argue and threaten each other. At that point, I asked why they did not arrest them. Their response was that they could not do such a thing because the two men had the right to fight. How about our right, I asked. We are hungry, I continued, and these men are violating our rights. We finally made it inside the restaurant to have our lunch. Upon returning to the meeting room, we had a good discussion on freedom and its limitations.

The last workshop took place in the city of Gjirokastra, the headquarters of the southern region of Albania where my village is located. The nearest city to my village is the smaller port city of Sarande just across from the island of Corfu. I knew this beautiful city as Saint Saranda[5] because it was named after a nearby ancient monastery that was dedicated to forty martyrs of the church. The communist regime had dropped the word *Saint* and the city continues to be called *Sarande*, with the ending *a* changed to an *e*. The head of the educational administration of the city invited me to go with them to Sarande and give a talk to the teachers in that area. I was delighted to accept the invitation. Following the meeting in the local high school, they took me for dinner to a fish restaurant outside the city. A nephew of mine approached and quietly informed me that the proprietor of the restaurant was the man from my village who was in charge of keeping track of my whereabouts during the communist regime. He was the one who informed the secret police that I was in Yugoslavia in 1971.

In closing this section, it should be emphasized that the workshops revealed a lot about Albanian teachers. There was much for them to learn about how to lead or even participate in a productive discussion. Speeches and lectures can be useful but they are not adequate for the development of concerned and active citizens. It was encouraging, however, that the teachers were attracted to open and interactive teaching presented to them. As they responded in writing, they wanted to have more workshops to assist them to get away from indoctrination and the politicization of education. The interactive approach to teaching appealed to them. They also expressed a desire for less central control and for more involvement on their part in making decisions at the local level about how to educate their students. It was obvious that Albanian teachers were committed to change. They were delighted that the project, known by now as the University of Washington (UW) project, was going to continue and that more opportunities would be provided for them to learn new ways to teach.

EXPLORING THE CURRICULUM

Where do we go from here? As soon as the meetings in Gjirokastra and Sarande were over, Dr. Wendling left for Corfu on her way back to the United States. I returned to Tirana to plan for the next phase of the project: the development of new social studies textbooks that would emphasize the teaching of democracy. It was soon discovered, however, that new textbooks for social studies were already under development. Besides, it became clear that there was no way a Balkan country would consent to have someone from the outside work on the country's textbooks. Such an undertaking was strictly a national matter. It has been that way for all Balkan nations since nationalism emerged during the mid-nineteenth century. This is an important dynamic in the Balkans that needs further elaboration.

The Balkan peoples lived together for centuries under the influence of the Romans. When the Roman Empire was divided into the Western Roman Empire and the Eastern Roman Empire, most of the Balkan peoples fell under the influence of the Eastern

Roman Empire. During and after the sixth century of current epoch, the Slavs moved into the area and dominated most of the Balkan Peninsula. At the same time, the Eastern Roman Empire evolved into the Byzantine Empire which was steeped in the Greek culture and the Eastern tradition of Christianity. As a result, the majority of the Balkan people joined that tradition which came to be known as the Eastern Orthodox Church. Finally, the Ottoman Empire destroyed the Byzantine Empire in 1454 and took over the entire area. The people were then organized in five groups (millets) on the basis of religion.[6] All Orthodox Christians, including those in the Balkan Peninsula, were grouped together under the leadership of the Patriarch[7] of Constantinople. The patriarch was responsible for order within the Orthodox, collected taxes, had authority on civil matters, and was directly accountable to the Sultan.

With the advent of nationalism, intellectuals from within the circles of the patriarchate were planning a revolution against the Ottoman Empire. They were not sure, however, with what to replace the Ottoman rule. Those closer to the patriarch, mainly Greeks, were thinking about creating a Christian nation that would encompass all the Orthodox people from the Balkans all the way to Egypt. But some of the non-Greek Balkan leaders did not agree with that notion. As a result, and motivated by nationalism, the Greeks established Greece, the Serbs Serbia, and so on. As already mentioned, the Albanians were the last to apply their nationalism with a demand for independence.

Although the revolutionaries were creating new nations, they were also trying to develop a distinct identity for their own nation—Serbian, Bulgarian, Romanian, and other. They did this because the peoples of the Balkan Peninsula, most of them uneducated peasants, were confused about their identity. The Turks and those from the Balkan Peninsula who joined Islam, like most of the Albanians and the Bosnians, were clearly identified as Muslims, but the rest of their subjects referred to themselves as Jews or Christians. The Greeks were also identified as Christians, but mostly they would refer to themselves as *Romaioi* or *Romioi*. As a result, the people were indifferent to the ethnic identities proposed by the various nationalist revolutionaries. No wonder, then, when two individuals in the still Turkish-held city of Thessaloniki were asked, very early in the twentieth century, whether they were

Romaioi (Greek) or Bulgarian, they responded with hesitation as follows: "Well, we're Christians—what do you mean *Romaioi* or *Voulgaroi*?"[8]

Due to the confusion, the leaders in each emerging nation had to invent a new identity and make it acceptable to their people. To accomplish this, they had to construct a national history that would match the new identity. Special councils were established to accomplish this objective. Quite often, they would not hesitate to violate well-established historical truths to support their conclusions. Though these practices go back more than one hundred years, they still prevail in the Balkans, especially when it pertains to the development of history and the social studies curricula. The communist regimes continued the practice as they were trying to promote an identity based strictly on the communist ideology.

Under the circumstances just described, the idea of developing social studies or civic education textbooks as an objective for the UW project was abandoned. Instead, our attention was turned at this point toward advising the Social Studies Curriculum Committee of the Pedagogical Research Institute to consider modeling textbooks from well-established democracies. In my conversations with the members of the committee, I was satisfied that they were consulting such textbooks, including those brought back from the United States by the members of the Ministry of Education group. The director of the Pedagogical Research Institute was a member of that group. As the discussion continued, it became evident that the Albanians were not in favor of the American model of textbooks where all related subjects were intergraded into what came to be known as social studies. They preferred, especially, to keep history and geography as separate subjects. They were willing, however, to develop a separate civic education program for grades one to ten that would be oriented toward the teaching of democracy. As it will be shown in later chapters, at least one course per grade would be devoted exclusively to some aspect of the democratic way of life. What would be the content of these courses?

As the curriculum discussion went on, the emphasis shifted to the content of the books for grades one through ten. I wanted to make sure that the exploration of social issues would be included in the books along with the basic concepts of democracy. Students at all levels must learn how to analyze an issue or problem, consider alternative solutions to the problem, weigh the consequences of each solution through discussion, and try to reach a consensus as to what might be the best solution. That is the reasonable way to deal with differences in a democracy. At some point in the discussion, I tried to give an example of an appropriate issue for an advanced grade. I used the issue related to Kosovo at that time—whether Serbia should continue controlling Kosovo, a region overwhelmingly populated by Albanians. After articulating the differences between the Albanian and Serbian positions, a very deep voice interrupted and let me know that there was no issue as far as Kosovo was concerned—the solution was only one, favoring complete independence for Kosovo. Obviously, I chose the wrong example. It is well known by now that Kosovo already declared its independence from Serbia.

Regardless of the above incident, the discussions proved to be fruitful. The development of a civic education curriculum was in the right direction. I was convinced that the American and Western European models would lead the committee to choose appropriate content for teaching democracy. At the same time, my initial notion to stay in the background and let Albanians emerge as the key builders of democracy in their country was significantly reinforced. The civic education curriculum was in progress, and the Ministry of Education had the ability to produce the related textbooks. But would the teachers be able to switch from propaganda to open and interactive teaching? This was the critical question that led the UW project to its next phase.

3

Selecting Leaders and Defining Basic Concepts

Selecting and Training the Leadership Team

It is again emphasized that one of the most critical guidelines of the project was to democratize Albania from within. The leadership of the democratization activities within the country had to come from Albania. To make this possible, we submitted another proposal to the United States Information Agency to fund the next phase of the project. The proposal was approved and work on this phase began in the fall of 1995. The first step was to select and appropriately prepare a leadership team consisting of four Albanian scholars/educators.

To find these individuals we had to look beyond the communist-influenced system. Under this system those who studied physics and mathematics were highly regarded and, therefore, occupied the best positions in the country. People with such a background, however, would not be the most appropriate for this project. Instead, the project needed scholars with a strong background in the social sciences and pedagogy, skill in writing, and an open mind. We also decided that none of those currently working in the Ministry's Textbook Publishing House would be appropriate at this stage of the project. The concern was that they might be too set in their ways in the development of educational materials. We insisted, therefore, that they send us social scientists and pedagogues from the Pedagogical Research Institute of Tirana and the country's various universities. We also needed individuals who spoke English, since neither I nor anyone else at the University of Washington spoke Albanian.

In view of the above facts, we requested four scholars who spoke English, were good writers, and had an academic background in social sciences and/or pedagogy. The last criterion was that the individuals selected were to be interviewed and accepted by the Director of the American Embassy's Cultural Office. This did not mean, of course, that the Embassy personnel were controlling the project. Instead, we requested their assistance to ensure that those selected spoke English and met the criteria relating to their scholarship and academic background. The persons selected were Drs. Mariana Sinani and Fatmira Myteberi from the Pedagogical Research Institute, Dr. Milika Dhamo from the University of Tirana, and Dr. Tonin Gjuraj from the University of Shkodra.

As soon as the selections were made, the individuals from the Minstry's Textbook Publishing House complained of being left out. Others were unhappy simply because they were not chosen. As the Director of the University of Washington (UW) project, I tried to explain the selection criteria and elaborated on our reason for bypassing the Textbook Publishing House. I explained that we wanted to prevent prior experience from affecting the development of new instructional materials. We also pointed out that there would be plenty of opportunities for all of them to play a part. Regardless, I was informed later that some tried to sabotage the project by sending letters to the funding agency. This action motivated by self-interest on the part of certain individuals put the entire project at risk. Fortunately, the officers in the funding agency ignored these letters thanks to the support of the project by the Cultural Office of the American Embassy in Tirana.

The above caused delays that forced us to revise our schedule. We had initially planned for the scholars to arrive in Seattle by October 5, 1995, participate in a training workshop, and then attend the annual meeting of the National Council for the Social Studies (NCSS) in Chicago. The duration of the stay was to be approximately two months. The program included theoretical input on democracy and democratic citizenship education for three weeks. A discussion was then to follow, ending with recommendations for the development of instructional materials. We were also hopeful that we could actually begin creating some of the materials. Unfortunately, because of the delays this plan was altered and the scholars arrived in Chicago on November 8, 1995, just in time to begin their experience in the United States with the NCSS meeting between November 9 and 12, 1995.

During the four days of the NCSS meeting, the Albanian scholars attended a number of sessions and participated in discussions on civic education. One of the sessions was organized by University of Washington faculty members. It consisted of a series of presentations, and subsequent discussions, under the title Democratic Citizenship Education and Multicultural Education at a Crossroads. We selected the sessions in advance and followed each one of them with discussions between the participants and invited guests. This approach gave the participants an opportunity to meet a number of prominent social studies educators in the United States, mainly experts in civic education and the development of relevant instructional materials. At the participant's recommendation, a number of these individuals were later invited to the University of Washington to provide input to the participants on civic education. Just as the Albanian Ministry officials earlier, the participants discovered that one of the most significant aspects of the NCSS meeting was the opportunity it provided to visit the exhibits of social studies and civic education instructional materials. They met authors and developers and accumulated numerous copies of textbooks and other materials to take with them back to Albania.

All indications were that the participants' experiences at the NCSS annual meeting were rewarding. We left Chicago on November 12 and upon arrival in Seattle the visitors were moved into two apartment units in a university dormitory. We spent the first two days familiarizing our guests with the university and the city of Seattle. We also visited an elementary school, along with another group of educators from Taiwan. We were reluctant to combine the Albanians and the Taiwanese because, years ago, Albania proposed the expulsion of Taiwan from the United Nations and the admission of China in its place. But there was no problem—the two groups had a great time together. This was especially evident later that evening when the two groups, along with several university professors, joined my wife and me for dinner at our home. It was a fun evening. The Albanians and the Taiwanese competed with each other singing popular songs from their country. The whole affair turned out to be a fabulous demonstration of good international relations. In fact, the Taiwanese invited the Albanians the next day for dinner at the Space Needle, the most famous landmark in Seattle.

The following two weeks of the workshop were devoted to providing input on three basic themes: (1) the concepts and processes of democracy; (2) democratic citizenship education; and (3) the development of civic education textbooks, teacher's guides, and other types of instructional materials with particular emphasis on the construction of interactive lesson plans. A number of scholars from throughout the United States were invited to make presentations and hold discussions with the participants. Among them were Professor John Patrick of Indiana University, a constitutional scholar and an internationally known authority on democratic citizenship education; Mr. Stan Christodlous, Editorial Director of the Maze Corporation and the former Executive Editor in social studies of Silver Burdett and Ginn; and Professor Denisse Mateolli of Purdue University. Professor Mateolli was invited at the request of the participants after they attended one of her workshops on civic education at the NCSS meeting.

In addition to outside scholars, a number of University of Washington faculty members were also involved in the workshop. Professor James A. Banks, an authority on multicultural education, discussed with the participants the concept of diversity and its implications for education. Professor Francis P. Hunkins, a nationally recognized specialist in curriculum development, exposed the participants to the basic principles of curriculum development and provided alternatives to the topdown centralized model of curriculum. Professor Nathalie Gehrke, a leader in middle school education, described middle school civic education curriculum and emphasized the importance of the individual student differences in teaching. Professor Walter Parker, a profound thinker and writer in democratic citizenship education, and a social studies textbook writer, explained the process of developing a textbook series. He also discussed with the Albanian educators the basic concepts and processes of democratic citizenship education in the United States.

Identifying the Basics of Democracy

Following the presentations and the related discussions during the two previous weeks, the rest of the time, except for a break due to

Thanksgiving, was devoted to meetings with the Albanian scholars under my direction. The objective of these meetings was to recount what was learned and identify the basics of democracy and democratic citizenship education. In other words, we wanted to determine what the participants learned that would be important for them to take back to Albania to assist them with the democratization of the country. The following themes emerged as an outline: (1) definition of democracy, (2) the relationship between democracy and education, (3) the historical perspective of democracy, (4) the basic principles of democracy, (5) the basic values of democracy, (6) the basic people skills of democracy, and (7) the impact of the basics of democracy on the various institutions of Albanian society. Each one of these themes will be briefly elaborated in the following paragraphs.

Defining democracy was not an easy task. Though the Albanian scholars recognized some basic concepts as being critical for the definition of democracy, they saw variations in the different existing democratic systems around the world. They also saw variations of democracy during the different historical periods. For example, there was the Athenian democracy, on the one hand, where all citizens participated in the decision-making process. On the other hand, there is representative democracy where a limited number of individuals are elected by the people to make important decisions on their behalf. Confusing as this may be trying to define democracy, the group clearly recognized that democracy is unthinkable without the idea of freedom—freedom of mind and soul, as they termed it. There can be no democracy without respect for the freedom of the individual. Democracy, they concluded, is the institutionalization of freedom. They saw it as something different than an ideology. Ideologies are closed, they argued. An ideology defines the goals and the means for reaching those goals. Democracy, on the other hand, is more open-ended. The people define the goals and the means to achieve them within a social context of freedom.

The participants also saw a role for education in developing and sustaining democracy. People in a democracy need a general education to acquire knowledge and develop the ability to make sound judgments. They also need to be instructed in civics to learn the basic principles of democracy and develop the values and skills necessary for living in a democracy. More will be said on education, including civic education, in the next section of this chapter.

As they surveyed the history of democracy, as briefly outlined in the introduction, the Albanians recognized the fragile nature of the system. They were fully convinced that democracy can easily be pushed aside without a deliberate effort to nurture it. Though they found Athenian democracy imperfect for leaving out parts of society, they admired it as a system and recognized its potential to expand and include more people, as it did throughout the centuries. The Albanian scholars felt that the opportunity for their country, and the entire Balkan Peninsula, to become democratic has arrived. They were convinced about this because they watched the people in their country and region being frustrated and uneasy, just as the people were during the Enlightenment period in Europe. As a result, they demonstrated a strong feeling that they suffered enough without freedom and human rights, especially under totalitarian communism. The review of democracy's history convinced the Albanian scholars that when people reach such a point the realization of democracy is a strong possibility.

The more the group engaged in discussion, the more they felt privileged at the prospect of playing a key role in democratizing their country. In preparation for that role, they were anxious to identify the basic principles, values, and skills of democracy. They saw these three elements as the basic materials with which to build the structure of democratic society. They wanted to understand them well and put them in a book that would serve as the basic manual for promoting democracy. This book was to be addressed mainly to practicing teachers, but also to politicians, civil servants, and as many as possible of the ordinary people. This book will be described in more detail toward the end of this chapter. At this point, the principles, values, and skills of democracy, as articulated by the Albanian scholars/educators, will be listed and briefly defined. It is interesting to notice that the Albanian scholars did not hesitate to occasionally contrast these basic elements of democracy with the realities of the communist system in Albania. Their preference for democracy was evident.

Basic Principles of Democracy

These principles address mainly the nature of society—the way the people relate with each other, and the way the government and the people relate with each other. As articulated by the Albanian educators, they are as follows:

Majority Rules with Protection of Minorities: None is left out or discriminated in any way. It is the responsibility of the government to protect minorities. As already pointed out elsewhere in this book, Albania does have a number of minorities that were suppressed by the communist regime. Nationalist tendencies played a part on this as well.

The Consent of the Governed: In a democracy, the people as a whole hold the supreme power. They elect the government. This is a new dynamic for a country in which the Communist Party had all the power.

Government Is Limited: The power of a government is limited through the separation of powers in the executive, the legislative, and the judicial branches. The first two have clearly spelled out functions in a constitution that has been approved by the people. The judiciary is independent of the other two branches and makes sure the provisions of the constitution are not violated. This is a fundamental change for Albania. Fifty years of communist dictatorship with all power in the hands of a few makes it difficult for elected leaders to accept limits on the government's power. As a result, the independence of the judiciary is often compromised by the executive branch. Even now, more than eighteen years after the first open elections, a lack of judicial independence continues to be a serious problem in Albania.

Open Society: People are free to express themselves and there are no restrictions of assembly. Each individual is free to have any political or religious affiliation. There are no restrictions on travel within or outside the country. The mass media are free and have an obligation to inform the people about the activities of the government. An open society is a new experience for Albanians, a situation to which they have to adjust.

Human Dignity and the Sanctity of the Individual: It is the individual and not the state that is the central focus of the system. Each individual has rights that cannot be arbitrarily violated by government authorities.

Sovereignty of the Law and Due Process: None is above the law in a democracy. All citizens must enjoy the right of equal protection under the law regardless of ethnic background, religious affiliation, or political orientation. The right of due process is fundamental in a democracy. People cannot just be arrested and thrown in jail without due process. This is a significant change for Albania where people were jailed or even executed for relatively minor offenses.

Basic Values of Democracy

Values consist mainly of beliefs the people have about themselves as individuals, the goals they set for themselves to guide them in life, and the way they wish to be treated by others and the government. The values identified were as follows:

Human Rights of Each Individual: Included among the most important rights of the individual are life, liberty, and the pursuit of happiness. The Albanians made sure to include the right to own property, something that was not allowed in communist Albania for more than fifty years.

The Common Good: The freedom of the individual in a democracy needs to be tempered by giving considerable attention to the common good. It is the only way to achieve a healthy social environment within which the individual can pursue his or her happiness. The common good, however, will have to be determined collectively by the people through dialogue rather than dictated by an individual or a particular group, as was the practice with communist regimes, including Albania's. As illustrated earlier in this book, people in Albania get confused when they hear that the common good is valued in a democracy.

The confusion rests on the fact that for fifty years the Albanians were forced to work hard for the benefit, as they were told, of the common good. That common good, however, was defined by a few, and it was only for the benefit of the state and those few who controlled it.

Justice: Basically, justice means fairness and due process of law. Government must be fair to each individual, and each individual must be fair to each other. Justice demands the application of the golden rule—*do unto others as you would have them do unto you.* As it was already pointed out, the individual is more important than the state. That was not the case in Albania for more than fifty years.

Equality: The Albanian scholars referred to the equality that was forced upon them by the totalitarian communist system as a "corrupt form of justice." Democracy calls for equality of opportunity rather than imposed equality of conditions and incomes. Individuals vary in their capacity and should be encouraged to use their creativity and their talents to pursue their happiness, so long as the ways they do it are fair to others.

Diversity: The world is getting smaller and people move and mix more than ever before. Diversity is a condition that is difficult to avoid. Differences in a society should be respected but a core of common values should also be pursuit vigorously. Not just diversity, but diversity in unity, provided unity is not perceived to be conformity. Just as any contemporary society, Albania is characterized by a full range of diversity based on individuals' regions, ethnicities, religions, languages, values, and customs.

Truth and Transparency: The Albanian people were totally isolated from the rest of the world for more than fifty years. Those in charge preferred to keep them from knowing about progress and the ways of life in other countries, especially in the neighboring countries that were outside the communist block. As our visiting scholars wrote, "truth was too often sacrificed." This was done to keep the people from dreaming for a better way of life. No wonder the Albanian people were shocked when the borders were forced open and they found out how far behind they were in terms of progress. Truth and transparency are valued in a democracy because they build trust in relationships, whether these relationships are between individuals or between the people and their government. Truth and transparency require openness and mass media that seek and report the truth rather than serving particular narrow interest.

Rational Patriotism: Patriotism is usually associated with nationalism and the idea of supporting one's country regardless of whether it is good or bad. Our visitors condemned this type of patriotism as "nationalistic chauvinism." But there is another kind of patriotism that was so well demonstrated by the fathers of the American system. They not only fought in battle to defend their country, but they also raised questions about their country to ensure it continued to improve in serving the common good of all the people. Wars are not good but they are occasionally forced on us. When that happens, we need to be patriotic enough to defend our country. However, the need to play a part in improving our country is always present. It is important to recognize that this type of patriotism is the lifeline of a democratic system. Everyone in such a system needs to demonstrate this type of patriotism.[1]

Basic Skills of Democracy

Democracy respects differences, but differences do often lead to conflicts in the relationships between people or groups of people. The underlying issues causing these conflicts need to be sorted out, and the conflicts must be fairly resolved with a solution that is guided by logic and the common good. A number of specific skills are critical in this process:

Rational Dialogue: It is to the advantage of all members of a society to try together to articulate the common interests, and through them, to reach for the definition of the common good. This process requires the resolution of issues, which in turn, raises the quality of association among people to a higher level. Such an achievement minimizes the effect of any differences that may exist. This is a critical process in a society, and the way to do it is through a civil and rational dialogue. Dialogue demands openness and the need for those involved to listen to each other with respect and civility.

Weighing Alternative Positions and Resolutions: The existence of an issue or a problem is the result of a variety of views or positions on a particular situation. Instead of fighting to see who will prevail, everyone concerned should talk civilly about their positions on the issue or problem. Then, weigh the consequences of each proposed solution using logic and the common good as guides.

Compromise: A winner-takes-all attitude is not a healthy approach to the resolution of differences. Such an approach pushes people farther apart. Democracy favors compromise. Meeting somewhere midway is the best way to make progress toward a better society.

Adjusting to New Situations: When a compromise is reached, a new dynamic emerges. The compromise might not be pleasing to everyone, but all have to go along with it and adjust to it. If it was done fairly, this is the best way to serve the common good. The skill of adjusting to new situations is especially important for Albanians at this point of their history. They lived for too long under different circumstances which forced them to be concerned only about their own narrow interests. The common good as defined by all requires them to change orientation, a development that calls for various adjustments.

Civic Skills: If the above skills are the stones and bricks for building a democracy, the civic skills are the mortar that holds democracy together. Respecting others, tolerating them, being courteous to them, and listening to them while they are talking are some of these skills.[2]

Satisfied with their understanding of the basic concepts and processes of democracy, the Albanian scholars asked for an additional discussion session to explore how these concepts and processes would be applied to the various social groups and institutions in Albania. Included among them were the family, religion, education, government, economy, and mass media. They saw the family and the various religious groups as sources for values compatible with democratic values. The family provides many opportunities for the individual to learn, for example, how to care for others and how to resolve differences. Religion usually teaches love for all human beings and respect for the worth and dignity of each individual. Consequently, the scholars concluded that, when family and religion promote such values, they are compatible with and supportive of democracy.

Regarding the application of democratic concepts to their government, the Albanians saw it as an instrument of the people rather than as an opportunity for some to serve their own interests. "As Albanian citizens," they wrote, "it is significant for us to realize that the mentality about government has changed. Government no longer serves the interests of those in government at the expense of the individual and society as a whole."[3] This statement implies significant changes. Drastic changes in the economic system are also implied by the Albanian scholars when they call for a return to economic freedom. They define economic freedom as "freedom to produce whatever one feels is needed in the market, freedom to buy and sell, freedom to compete, freedom to secure profit, freedom to own property, and freedom to choose a job."[4] The Albanians were deprived of these freedoms for too long.

Finally, the Albanian scholars called for the mass media to be free and to concentrate on the following functions: (1) provide information on all sides of the various issues, (2) provide information to the public that is characterized by impartiality and lack of bias, and (3) play a role in monitoring the activities of the government at all of its dimensions and levels.

IDENTIFYING THE BASIC ELEMENTS OF DEMOCRATIC CITIZENSHIP EDUCATION

When the communists took over in Albania, I was in the elementary school. They would do anything to separate us children from our parents and the beliefs for which they stood. School was less challenging and more fun after the communists took control. For the most part, the teachers involved us in dramatic play demonstrating the struggle of the communists against the existing order. The communists were always the winners. Our parents privately objected to this practice, but they were reluctant to reveal this to us. They were afraid that we might tell the teacher about their disagreement, which could have led to their arrest and imprisonment.

In fact, I recall one time when I needed my father's *foustanela*, a traditional Greek garment dating back to the Greek war of independence, to appear in a play. It was the garment my father wore when he married my mother, who kept it in a chest with other valuables. I asked her for it and she refused to give it to me. I cried for it but she continued to refuse. Finally I threatened her that I was going to tell my teacher about her refusal. She immediately opened the chest and gave me the foustanela. She knew that she could have been arrested.

The communists knew that if they were to succeed in establishing the new order, they had to go through the schools. What they implemented, however, was propaganda and not education. In a democracy, propaganda as a form of education is unacceptable because it promotes a closed system with goals and methodologies that are predetermined by an individual or a group of individuals. Even politicized education is not appropriate for a democracy because it often leads to advocating only the views of the political party in power. In a democracy, the people decide on the goals and methodologies of their system. Being an open system, democracy requires an open education, an education that respects knowledge above all and relies entirely on the rational process to arrive at conclusions. Even the development and acquisition of beliefs goes through the scrutiny of the rational process in a democratic system.

Open liberal education is a must for a democratic society. At the same time, a democratic society needs civic education—not the totalitarian type of civic education that is based on obedience but the democratic type of civic education that is based on freedom, reason, and voluntary acceptance. To avoid confusion, we decided in our discussions with the Albanian educators to refer to civic education as *democratic citizenship education*. The following section briefly presents the basic elements of this type of education as they were articulated during our discussions. The elements consist of (1) objectives, (2) curriculum, and (3) teaching methodology.

Democratic Citizenship Education Objectives

As these objectives were articulated, the Albanian educators took into consideration the basic principles, values, and skills of democracy as presented earlier. They also considered the Albanian pre-university education law of June 1995, Article 1, which spells out the goals of compulsory education in their country. Included among the objectives are the acquisition and/or development in students of the following:

Knowledge: This includes basic concepts and generalizations that describe the nature and conditions of a particular society. It is emphasized here that in addition to settled and accepted conditions, the problems of society should also be included. The study of a society's problems can be controversial and is usually avoided. This is unfortunate. It deprives the students from acquiring a complete picture of their society. At the same time, it deprives them of the opportunity to deliberate on how the problems could be resolved. Deliberating on the problems gives the students excellent opportunities to prepare themselves for their role as citizens.

Values: A basic characteristic of a democracy is recognition of diversity. Commitment to diversity calls for diversity in values. This makes it difficult to decide what values to choose for teaching in schools. As a result, a value-free education was advocated in the United States following the civil rights movement of the sixties. It did not take very long, however, to realize that a society cannot exist without a set of common values. This realization generated a debate that led to the promotion of the basic values of democracy as the core of values to be taught in schools. As presented earlier in this chapter, these values are human rights of the individual, the common good, justice, equality, diversity, truth, and rational patriotism. These values should not, however, be perceived as absolute. In a democracy, people do have the right to make changes to existing values or adopt new ones.

Skills: Democracy is for the people and relies on them to sustain and improve it. It is imperative that the people actively participate in the democratic process. To do that, the schools must help them develop a set of skills. These skills, as articulated by the Albanian visitors, were presented earlier in this chapter. They are rational dialogue, weighing alternative positions and resolutions, compromise, adjusting to new situations, and civic skills.

Democratic Citizenship Education Curriculum

It must again be stressed that a curriculum for teaching democracy cannot be devoid of national elements. This is especially so in the Balkans where national identities were constructed after the various ethnic groups emerged from the Ottoman rule less than two centuries ago. In the case of Albania, this occurred less than one century ago. Whatever the national elements of the curriculum are, however, they should not violate the truth as revealed by sound history. Following is the outline of a democratic citizenship education curriculum that the Albanian scholars put together for their country. The content of the democratic citizenship education curriculum consists mostly of knowledge, but it is also intended to help children and youth develop democratic values and skills, mainly through the teaching methodologies they apply. It is a program for grades one through ten divided in three cycles as follows:

Grades One through Four: The content of the curriculum in these grades is oriented toward the socialization of children and is organized around the following themes: the children in the family, the children at school, the children in society, communication and the means of communication, and health and public environment.

Grades Five through Eight: The content in these grades addresses social, political, judicial, and economic aspects of society. It is organized around the following themes: nature and the role of the community, the rights and responsibilities of the citizen, relations between the individual and the government, the citizen and the law, and producers and consumers.

Grades Nine and Ten: The content of the curriculum in these two grades is to deepen the understanding of society and make the students aware of their role in society within the context of democratic citizenship. Included among the main themes for these grades are the following: family, culture, science and technology in an information society, sociopolitical and governmental organization of society, labor, deviant behavior in society, people and the environment, and Albania in international relations.

Democratic Citizenship Teaching Methodology

After a number of lectures and discussions on teaching methodology, as well as several observations in classrooms, the Albanian educators identified a number of basic principles related to effective teaching. These principles are as follows:

Effective Teaching Is Student Oriented: A student-oriented methodology implies recognition of the individual differences of the students. Teaching is done in ways that take these differences into consideration.

Effective Teaching Is Meaningful: What the students learn must mean something to them. One way to achieve this is by relating what is being taught to the life experiences of the students. Another way is to connect what the students learn with something they already know.

Effective Teaching Is Challenging to Students: Meaningful content is challenging, but the students can be further challenged by integrating the teaching and learning of content with the teaching and learning of values and skills. A good example of teaching in an integrated manner is by turning the classroom into a laboratory for learning democracy. For instance, the students learn democratic principles and values by using their classroom as a laboratory to determine how well they implement such principles and values. Do they respect each other? Do they appreciate diversity? Do they resolve their classroom problems through civil dialogue? Do they compromise? Do they take responsibility for improving their classroom environment? Such questions can be challenging to students and lead to lasting learning. The community, the state, and even the world can also be used as laboratories depending on the level of the students.

Effective Teaching Is Interactive: Students learn not only from the teacher but they also learn from each other, and by themselves. Students learn better when they participate in the learning process rather than having a teacher always lecturing to them. Interactive teaching and learning require good planning on the part of the teacher.

DEVELOPING THE MANUAL FOR DEMOCRATIC CITIZENSHIP EDUCATION

Following the experiences at the annual meeting of NCSS and the three weeks of input and discussions, I was absolutely convinced that the authorities in Albania sent me the best people for the task ahead. Milika Dhamo, Tonin Gjuraj, Fatmira Myteberi, and Mariana Sinani proved to be the most promising element for success in the democratization of Albania. They loved their country, they clearly recognized democracy as the best option for Albania, and they had the intellect and the character to assume the leadership for achieving that goal. They were also wonderful human beings. My colleagues at the university were fascinated with them and found them to be inspiring resources for them and their students. My wife, Maria, and our children adopted them as an extension to our family. From this point on, I started referring to my distinguished guests as the *leadership team* of the project.

We jointly decided that the next major objective would be to move toward the preparation of democratic citizenship education teachers. These teachers would be the agents for spreading democracy in every district of Albania through the educational system. This was a tremendous task and to accomplish it we needed the proper tools. The leadership team was now ready to begin writing the teacher's manual mentioned earlier in this chapter, consisting mainly of the basics of democracy and democratic citizenship education. This manual would serve as the basic instrument for the preparation of the teachers. It would also be used to inform society in general on democracy and democratic education. I decided not to become involved as an author or coauthor of the manual. Displaying a strong belief in the principle of democracy from within, I encouraged the members of the team to be the authors. I agreed, however, to serve as an advisor and editorial assistant.

The manual started with the development of an outline under the following chapter headings and subheadings:

Chapter 1: Albania Moves toward Democracy
The first three years: achievements and problems

The need for democratic citizenship education
The purpose of this manual
Chapter 2: The Basics of Democracy
Definition of democracy
Democracy and education
Democracy in the course of history
Basic principles of democracy
Basic values of democracy
Basic skills of democracy
Social groups/institutions and democracy
Chapter 3: The Basics of Democratic Citizenship Education
Basic principles of democratic citizenship education
The objectives of democratic citizenship education
The curriculum of democratic citizenship education
Methods of teaching democratic citizenship
Teacher education; needs and prospects

The process for developing the manuscript was not easy. Each participant assumed responsibility for writing a section of the manual in the Albanian language. Since there was still time before they left for Albania, they started writing. The enthusiasm with which they approached the task enabled them to make significant progress. They practically completed the manuscript before they left the United States on December 21, 1995. Soon after they arrived in Tirana, they were anxious to meet to discuss once more what they wrote and to coordinate their four portions into a single manuscript, which was done promptly.

The next step was for each one of the team leaders to translate their portion of the manuscript into English and send it to me. I put a considerable amount of time editing what was sent to me. Their English needed some attention but I was careful not to drastically change the wording. I made every effort to make sure the authors recognized their writing and identified with it. If I felt there was something missing in a statement or section, I would propose an addition or raise questions to help them fill the gap. Six months after they left Seattle, at the end of May 1996, I went to Albania to discuss my editing along with a number of other matters. There were a couple of minor points needing discussion but they were quickly resolved.

With the manuscript for the manual finally completed, we planned to publish it during the next funding cycle along with a series of teacher's guides that the leadership team started before they left Seattle. More details on the guides are presented in the next chapter.

4

Teaching, Learning, and Teacher's Guides

Switching from Propaganda to Interactive and Open Teaching and Learning

Since the responsibility for the development of the textbooks had already been assumed by the Ministry of Education, the University of Washington (UW) project turned its attention toward the development of teacher's guides that would accompany the textbooks. Teacher's guides were necessary to enable teachers to switch from lecturing and propaganda to interactive and open teaching based on knowledge, reason, dialogue, and consensus. We realized that this switch would not be easy to accomplish as the teachers had grown up in a system where knowledge was restricted, and intimidation and fear were considered appropriate methods for reaching predetermined politico-ideological objectives. This was just as true in the schools as it was in society in general. The teachers would use methods and activities that would make the school a fun place to be. Sports and dramatic plays, for example, were very important. If that did not work, however, the teachers would not hesitate to use intimidation and fear to achieve their objectives.

Having lived in Albania during the early stages of the communist takeover, I still recall vividly some of the methods used in the schools. For example, the students in my school were organized in a military fashion to resemble the partisans[1] who fought against the Nazis. We were divided into three units and each one of these units was headed by a student selected from the upper grades. I do not know why, but I was selected to be the commander of all three units in my school. It may have been because I lost three years of school as a result of World War II and so I was older than the other children. Or, I may have been selected because my father was a priest and the communists wanted to get me away from his influence. As I recall, the education authorities sent us, the "officers," decorations and a briefcase from the nearby city. My decorations consisted of three red stars, while each one of my fellow officers had one. We wore the stars on our shirt sleeve. We would put them on and carry our briefcase across our shoulder, just as the real military officers did.

Every morning, we would line up the students in three rows in front of the main entrance to the school and each one of my three one-star subordinates would call their row to attention and proceed with the roll-call. When all three of them finished, they would take turns reporting to me after saluting by raising their right arm in a clenched fist, the typical military salute of the communists. I would then turn around behind me where the principal stood, salute him, give the report on attendance, and ask for his permission to order the students to march toward their classrooms. It was quite a spectacle and adults would usually gather around watching us. Some would find the event interesting while others would watch it for a while and move away shaking their head. In the beginning, all the students were fascinated by the whole affair, especially those of us with decorations and authority. It did not take very long, however, for things to happen that led to intimidation and threats.

One day during recess, all four of us officers took a walk toward the main spring of the village not very far from the school. A few yards from the spring were several workers building a house. We stopped to watch them. They took a good look at us and stopped working. They were just looking at us without saying anything. Finally, one of them looked around to make sure no one else was listening and let us have it. In a very disapproving voice he asked, "What are those decorations?" Before we had a chance to say anything, he scolded us for being drawn to such things and not concentrating on our studies. It was time to go back to our classes, and we started walking away toward the school. We had our heads down thinking about the encounter with the construction workers. Immediately my father came to my mind; a mild and wise man. He never said anything about my decorations, but I was certain he was not approving of them. I felt guilty and very confused. As soon as I walked in the classroom, I took off my decorations, attached them to the briefcase, and handed everything to my teacher. Somewhat surprised and concerned, the teacher asked, "What is this?" "I am resigning," I said and quietly went to my seat.

The next day, the whole school was brought into the largest classroom of the school. I knew what was going to happen. Every time the teachers noticed something they did not like, they would deal with it publicly. They would bring everyone in the school together for a sort of confession and accusation session. They called it a self-criticism session. Even the inspector from the nearby city, a former teacher of mine, was there this time. Following the usual procedure, the principal asked whether anyone had anything to confess. They expected me to confess about my resignation, but I did not do it. No one else stood up to confess anything either. There was complete silence in the room. As it was always the case, the principal stood up and asked whether there was anyone wishing to criticize someone else. One of my classmates came forward and criticized me for resigning. The inspector immediately stood up and asked me for the reasons for my resignation. Fortunately for the construction workers, I chose to simply say that I did not like to wear the decorations. He dismissed my reason and continued pressing me to the point where he threatened me with arrest. Finally, he looked at me in a serious way and shouted that I could be executed. At that point, I burst into a nervous laugh. I was afraid, but I was not able to say or do anything other than to just laugh mechanically. He left me alone and the session ended.

In retrospect, I am thankful for not implicating anyone because executions, many of them public, were a common occurrence at that time. It was one of the methods the authorities used to make people comply with the ways of the new system. I witnessed a public execution myself as a teenager. A man was brought to our village to be tried for attempting to escape to Greece. The judge came from some other place accompanied by about a couple hundred soldiers. As soon as he arrived, he set up his court in the front yard of the village church and requested that all the people of the village gather in front of him. The soldiers were congregated to his right, while the man to be tried was to his left with his hands tied behind his back. It did not take the judge very long to read the accusation and ask the gathering to indicate by voice whether the man on trial should be executed. A thunderous "yes" came from the crowd, mainly the soldiers. The man was immediately led to the tree from which the church bell was hanging and was shot to death right in front of all of us. Everyone was then ordered to line up and walk by the man's bloody dead body. I will never forget that scene, which was obviously created to intimidate all of us in the village. As the regime settled, executions did not happen as often and as open to the public, but intimidation, arrests, severe punishment, and propaganda continued until the regime was overthrown in the early nineties.

Considering this background, it was absolutely necessary to prepare the teachers to think and teach differently. That is why we decided to develop the teacher's guides. Our plan was to use the guides to train the teachers and then give a guide to each one of them to continue using it in his or her teaching. Before elaborating on the teacher's guides, however, a brief discussion on teaching and learning as well as how they relate to each other is appropriate.

Let me start by emphasizing that teaching and learning go together. One may argue that such a relationship between these two processes is obvious. Reality indicates, however, that this is not the case. There is plenty of teaching taking place, in just about every society, but the amount of learning varies considerably. In some cases learning is adequate but in a disturbing number of other cases very little learning is taking place. What good is teaching if the students do not learn? Consequently, it is important that educators make sure teaching is deliberately linked to the learning of predetermined objectives. If learning is not taking place or is not taking place at adequate levels, teaching will have to be adjusted.

Learning should not be viewed, of course, only in terms of the acquisition of knowledge. As already pointed out in the previous chapter, learning should also include the development of intellectual skills, socially desirable values, and acceptable behavioral skills and habits. Values, skills, and habits are especially important in the field of civic education. Such a broad view of learning requires a multifaceted kind of teaching that goes beyond lecturing and filling the blank spaces on a worksheet. It requires the kind of teaching that invites the involvement of the students in the learning process.

There are those who may argue that teaching values is indoctrination or propaganda similar to that practiced in Albania during the communist regime. There is, however, a difference. The communists would do anything, especially with the children, to convince learners to believe in their ideology. They would not hesitate to lie or distort the facts to achieve their objectives. A good example is an experience I had in my village during my childhood. Each village had a person known in the Greek language as the *diafotistis* (enlightener). This person would go around trying to convince people to forget the old ways and believe in the communist ideology. He approached me one day during lent and offered me a piece of candy. I refused it because I was fasting during lent. I was supposed to stay away from meat and dairy products for forty days. I was taught by my father, a priest in the Orthodox Church, that candy was not allowed during lent because butter was used in making it. Then the enlightener asked me, "Why do we have lent?" Unable to respond, I suggested that he should go and ask my father. He replied by offering to tell me how lent was started. When Jesus was alive, he said, he had a huge farm and one year the farm produced a lot of onions. Jesus tried to sell the onions but only few bought them. Consequently, he told the people to fast so that he could sell his onions. The story made some sense to me, more so than some of the miracles my father was telling us about in Sunday school.

Teaching methods that do not respect knowledge and the rational process have no place in a democratic society, even when values are taught. Teaching democratic values cannot be done with lies and distortion of facts. Teaching values in a democratic society respects the truth and uses the rational process to convince the students to accept, modify, or even reject a particular value. A review by the leadership team of the various teaching models revealed that *interactive teaching* is the most promising model for involving students in the process of achieving educational objectives needed in a democracy. Interactive teaching provides opportunities for the students to learn from the teacher as well as from each other. It also encourages them to learn by themselves.

It should be emphasized that the teaching and learning of knowledge objectives play a strategic role in interactive teaching. As the students are taught knowledge in the form of concepts and generalizations, they interact with the teacher and among themselves. Through that process, they learn how to search for information, discuss it, and put it together to reach conclusions. Such a process helps the students to go beyond memorization. At the same time, interactive teaching promotes a classroom environment in which the students observe and practice democratic values and skills. As they advance their knowledge and develop skills and values, the students gain a rounded education and strengthen their capacity to live effectively in a democratic society.

DEVELOPING INTERACTIVE LESSON PLANS FOR TEACHER'S GUIDES

As mentioned earlier, the original plan was for the project to assist Albania to develop new civic education textbooks. The design of these textbooks would have incorporated elements that would have made it possible for the teachers to teach content through the application of the interactive approach to teaching. Since the Ministry of Education was already on its way developing the textbooks, the leadership team decided to develop teacher's guides to ensure the application of interactive teaching and the involvement of the students in the learning process.

Before the four members of the leadership team left for Albania, we agreed that each one of them would assume the responsibility for the development of a manuscript for a teacher's guide to the textbook of a particular grade between grades four through seven. The teacher's guides would be in the form of lesson plans, one for each lesson in the assigned textbook. The work would be done in Albania in the Albanian language. Each lesson would then be translated in the English language so that I would be able to review them and make suggestions for any adjustments.

Before the team left Seattle, however, it was necessary to design a model of a lesson plan to provide for a degree of uniformity throughout the series of lesson plans. The following is a typical outline of a lesson plan that emerged from the discussions the team had, along with brief explanations and at least one example from a fifth-grade lesson plan:

Objectives: The objectives have to be student-oriented rather than just showing what content will be covered. Following the teaching of a lesson, the students should be able to demonstrate, mainly through application, what new learning they have acquired—a concept, a value, an intellectual or social skill, or a combination of them. For example, an objective from a fifth-grade lesson plan may read as follows: "Students will be able to identify various roles people play in life and divide these roles into temporary and permanent."

Motivational Activity: The teacher should think of a clever way to draw the students into the lesson. One way to do it would be to connect the theme of the lesson with the students' everyday life. The author of the fifth-grade plan recommended that the teacher ask the students to indicate on a piece of paper the places of work that they visited recently and the reason for which they visited these places. By doing so, the teacher leads the students through questions and discussion to the concept of roles in life and their variety.

Lesson Development Activities: A variety of teaching strategies could be applied here for the development of the lesson. The leadership team identified several of these strategies, such as questioning, cooperative learning, group research, group discussion, role playing, conflict resolution, and decision making. For example, the author of the fifth-grade lesson plan used the questioning strategy to lead the students to an understanding of the importance of everyone in society taking their professional role seriously. Included among the questions used by the author to assist the students toward this objective were the following: How would you react if you went to the hospital and most of the employees were sitting around chatting with each other while drinking coffee or were watching football on television? Would you get the treatment you needed? Would you consider such behavior on the part of the hospital employees to be appropriate and fair? Another activity used in the sample plan was to have the students make a list of roles people play during a brainstorm session and then separate the temporary roles from those that are permanent.

Evaluation: The emphasis in evaluation should be on determining the difference a new learning made in students. Do they know something they did not know before? Do they feel different? Did they develop a deeper appreciation of something taught? Can they apply a skill they just developed? In the case of the sample lesson plan, it asks whether the students express an appreciation for people who show commitment to what they do professionally. Remember, it takes time to evaluate whether a student developed a particular value or not. One exposure to a particular value is not enough, unless it happened in a dramatic way.

Assignments: For social studies and humanities, society is the laboratory. The best assignments are those asking the students to connect a new learning with real situations. Synthesizing new with old learnings is also a good assignment. For example, having each student make a list of the roles their family members play in society and then divide the roles into temporary and permanent will assist them to deepen their understanding of the various roles people play. Activities such as this could lead the students to think about their own vocational orientation.

When I visited Albania at the end of May 1996, the members of the leadership team had made considerable progress toward the development of the manuscripts for the teacher's guides. They were very enthusiastic about their contribution. It was something new they were introducing in Albania and foresaw overwhelming acceptance by the civic education teachers. They still needed more time, however, to finish the work. As a result, we decided to request a six-month no-cost extension, which was eventually granted. In the meantime, we were planning for the development of teacher's guides for the rest of the grades. It was our dream to produce and publish a complete series of teacher's guides from grade one all the way to grade ten.

DEVELOPING ADDITIONAL TEACHER'S GUIDES THROUGH PARTNERSHIPS

As the development of the manual for democratic citizenship education and the teacher's guides for grades four through seven were progressing, the project was attracting attention. Before even the leadership team left Seattle, I was approached by the George Soros Foundation, a philanthropic organization based in Hungary, which was exploring the possibility of cooperating in the UW project. The George Soros Foundation had an extensive educational project in Albania known as the Albanian Educational Development Project (AEDP). This project emphasized the restructuring of the Albanian educational system based on democratic standards, including provisions for civic education. I was pleased to accommodate them. As we were in the midst of writing the manuscripts for the teacher's guides, I invited the director of the AEDP, Dr. David Avdul, to send someone to Seattle to learn more about the UW project. Dr. Avdul, an Albanian American, asked his brother Richard, a professor of Education at the University of St. Francis in Fort Wayne, Indiana, to travel to Seattle.

A delightful gentleman and a very engaging personality, Professor Richard Avdul joined us and instantly became a part of the group. We worked together as we were trying to finalize the nature and outline of the lesson plans for the teacher's guides. We also took time to familiarize him with the philosophy and the overall plans of the project. We described to him the planned manual on democratic citizenship education with its emphasis on the basics of democracy and democratic citizenship education. We also explained to him our decision to use the newly developed civic education textbooks by the Ministry of Education as the basis for the curriculum. Professor Avdul agreed with us that the teacher's guides would be the best way to have teachers involve the students in the learning process and ensure the development of democratic values and skills in addition to knowledge. He also agreed with our plans to train the teachers on the proper use of the teacher's guides. We had no funds for the publication of the materials or for any of our other plans but we were hoping the momentum generated by the project would enable us to secure the funds in order to keep moving forward.

Apparently, Professor Richard Avdul gave a good report to his brother David back in Albania. The AEDP agreed with his recommendation to join us in our effort to improve civic education in Albania. We were delighted to have them as partners because they had been in Albania for about five years and they were well established with an extensive network throughout the country. At my suggestion, they agreed to assume the responsibility for developing the manuscripts for the teacher's guides for grades one through three. Within a short period, a small group of Albanian educators were selected and sent to the University of St. Francis to work with Professor Avdul to accomplish the task. I was invited to

Fort Wayne, Indiana, and spend a couple of days with the group presenting the philosophy and plans of the UW project. It was important to emphasize to them the need for uniformity in the lesson plans throughout the grades. As a result, we spent some time discussing the format of the lesson plans as we developed it in Seattle. Professor Avdul made sure the guides for grades one through three were similar to those for grades four through seven.

Soon after I went to Albania in May 1996, Dr. David Avdul and I met for the first time. We worked well together solidifying and expanding our partnership. In addition to developing the manuscripts for grades one through three, the AEDP agreed to pay for the publication of these guides. They also agreed to share the cost for the publication of the rest of the teacher's guides and the manual for democratic citizenship education. Dr. Avdul even offered to pursue funding through the Soros Foundation for the anticipated training of the teachers in the proper implementation of the teacher's guides. Unfortunately, he left his position by the end of 1996 and was unable to act on his offer. The relationship with the AEDP continued, however, in a number of ways. Members of their staff specializing in social studies and civic education were participating in the planning of UW project activities and the charting of new directions. Two national conferences on civic education were eventually organized and carried out jointly. The capacity of the project leadership team was greatly enhanced by the partnership with the AEDP and the cooperation of some capable people in that organization, such as Barthul Musai, Vasilaq Zoto, and Zana Lita. It was a pleasure witnessing young professional scholars working together so successfully. All they needed was trust and freedom to create and demonstrate with confidence their capacity to make a difference.

The central offices of the AEDP in Tirana were quite impressive. They occupied an entire building in the central part of the city and the whole operation was well organized. I paid particular attention in the way they were handling their finances because I needed assistance in that area. During every trip in Albania, I carried in my briefcase thousands of dollars in cash. There was no place where money could be wired and then withdrawn as needed. Checks, even traveler's checks, were not widely used in Albania at that time. The Albanian financial institutions were in the process of being reorganized and were not yet perceived to be secure or trustworthy. It was neither safe nor practical to carry twenty to thirty thousand dollars in your briefcase to pay for various activities around the country, but I had to do it. My briefcase was always with me. I looked like the officer who carries the briefcase with the nuclear code when traveling with the US president. During the night, I would hide the briefcase not under my bed but under my pillow for more security.

Fortunately, I developed enough confidence in the AEDP to open an account with their financial division. During each trip I would deposit the money with them in a separate account and withdraw from it as needed. It worked well and I used that arrangement until reputable foreign banks established branches in Albania. Since I spoke Greek, I eventually opened an account with the Tirana branch of the National Bank of Greece. Whenever there was a need to make a distribution, I would deposit the amount budgeted for that need and withdraw from it as needed. In my absence, two of the team leaders were authorized to jointly withdraw money from the bank. All of these arrangements were done, of course, with the consent of the University of Washington and the approval of the funding agency.

Since we are in the area of finances, I should mention a difference that emerged between the AEDP and our project about how to finance the writing of the teacher's guides. We had approval from our funding agency to pay our authors a certain amount of money for each lesson plan developed. The AEDP was paying their authors less. As soon as I expressed the concern that the difference might lead to a problem, our project's leadership team offered to develop their lessons for a reduced amount. It should be noted here that the reason we paid our writers a little more was our project's policy to pay a fair amount, but only for work done to produce something or to provide a service. Due to low salaries, the preferred practice in Albania, at that time, was to be hired on a retainer basis and get paid per month. We avoided anything that could be perceived as an entitlement, but we provided a fair pay for work done. This was difficult in the beginning for some to accept, but eventually they recognized the fairness of the policy.

DEVELOPING NEW PROPOSALS AND COPING WITH REVOLT AND UNEXPECTED DELAYS

With the enthusiasm of all concerned, the project was moving forward. The manuscripts for the manual on democratic citizenship education and the teacher's guides for the first seven grades were about to be completed. A valuable partnership with the AEDP was established. Plans for the continuation of the project were in place. A new application was submitted to the U.S. government requesting funds to support a number of activities, including (1) publication of all completed manuscripts, (2) development of manuscripts for teacher's guides for grades eight through ten, (3) initiation of the process of training teachers, and (4) development of university-level textbooks for the preparation of future social studies and civic education teachers. The Albanian people continued to show their desire for democracy, and they were confident that forward movement in that direction was inevitable. Unfortunately, things were not going that well with their government and with politics in general.

The political and social events that were about to unfold in Albania over the next year would have an enormous negative effect on the UW project. Following the elections of 1992, the future of Albania appeared to be very bright. In anticipation of positive change, the international community, especially the United States of America, was supportive of the new government. The popularity of President Sali Berisha was high, and he appeared destined to become the modern Skanderbeg[2] of Albania. Unfortunately, for many reasons, it did not happen. Following the elections, President Berisha concentrated his efforts on achieving full control of the Democratic Party and strengthening the office of the president. By doing so, he alienated some of his original close allies to the point where they left the party and formed their own political parties in opposition to the Democratic Party. It is interesting to note that according to Miranda Vickers and James Pettifer, "this absolute concentration of government around the Presidency, has alienated the more liberal and European-minded elements of the original DP leadership, and has also led to bad decisions being taken."[3]

At the same time, corruption was suspected within the Democratic Party. As Biberaj pointed out, "party bosses in Tirana and at the district level held a tight grip over the distribution of public sector jobs to party stalwarts; helped supporters secure government benefits and services; helped new entrepreneurs obtain contracts, licenses, and credits; and so on."[4] In light of high unemployment and poverty in the country, such behavior on the part of the officials contributed in branding the government as corrupt, ineffective, and indifferent to the needs and concerns of the people. These feelings were reinforced by witnessing daily a troubling relationship between the government and the opposition parties. While each side was attacking the other, the basic issues of the country, such as land distribution, remained unresolved. Both sides were to blame because both were demonstrating a lack of understanding of democratic principles and processes. In Biberaj's words, "the new elites had no tradition of democratic problem solving, and a limited understanding of their rights and responsibilities. In a county steeped in authoritarianism," Biberaj continued, "they lacked a willingness to compromise, and relied on command rather than bargaining. The concept of accountability remained largely alien."[5]

While the above circumstances were unfolding, poverty and unemployment continued to increase and strikes started disrupting and paralyzing the country. Unable to calm the country through reforms, the government resorted to force. An extensive and powerful police force was established to deal with the strikes and establish law and order. As the time for new elections in 1996 was approaching, some positive initiatives were undertaken by the government but there were questions as to whether they were enough to ensure the reelection of Sali Berisha and his Democratic Party. The opposition was determined to work for a strong showing, especially after the government succeeded in modifying the election law in its own favor.

The elections took place as scheduled on May 26, 1996. My wife and I happened to be in Tirana at that time. We were staying at the Rogner Hotel where many of the international observers were staying. The spirits were high among the people as they were anticipating the results. As soon as the polls closed, the observers on their return to the hotel provided us with all kinds of stories concerning the conduct of the elections, including incidents of voter intimidation and other irregularities. Later in the evening, my wife and I went to our room and we heard commotion out in the streets and extensive gun shooting. The Democratic Party supporters were celebrating victory, and they were driving around town in groups shooting in the air. Not knowing what was happening, my wife was quite afraid. I reminded her that the hotel was quite safe, but I suggested that we lay on the floor away from the windows to avoid any stray bullets. The situation calmed down after a couple of hours, and we went to bed wondering what the next day was holding for us.

As we woke up and went downstairs for breakfast, we found out that the Democratic Party was declared the winner. The opposition did not accept the results as announced and declared that they would not participate in the parliament. Though the police had imposed a ban on demonstrations following the elections, the opposition parties defied the ban and on May 28 staged a massive demonstration in the central square of Tirana. The police attacked the demonstrators and used what the foreign media, still in Tirana, considered excessive force. This event and others that followed caused the government to lose the support of the international community, including that of the United States. Initially, the United States asked for reelections only in districts in which irregularities were observed. Not much later, however, Washington asked for the elections to be repeated throughout the country.

In the midst of this turmoil in the country, it was time for my wife and me to return to the United States. We decided to go by car to the Southern port city of Sarande, take a small boat across to Corfu, and from there fly to Athens on our way back to the United States. The car and a driver were kindly provided by the Pedagogical Research Institute of Tirana. Two of the project team leaders offered to accompany us until the city of Gjirokastra, approximately forty miles north of Sarande. The husband of one of the team leaders was a candidate for election from the city of Gjirokastra under the Socialist Party. I knew this man—a wise man—not as a politician but as a human being and friend. When his wife was in Seattle, he visited us in our home several times and we had some very delightful conversations, though neither of us spoke the language of the other. Someone would always offer to serve as our interpreter. Every time I was in Albania, we never failed to meet at least once for lunch or dinner, along with an interpreter. If it all was left up to the two of us, we were confident that the world would be a better place, while Albania would be a consolidated democracy a lot faster.

As we approached the Gjirokastra square, we found it full of policemen. Our plan was to have lunch together before my wife and me continuing our trip to Sarande. Our friend approached us quietly to inform me that he was not supposed to be in the square that day. He apologized and invited all of us to a restaurant toward the mountain away from the city. The restaurant was almost empty. We settled in a table next to the balcony door. All of a sudden, there was another car climbing toward the restaurant. Four men came out, walked into the restaurant, and sat in a table not far from ours. I was not sure, but if someone had asked me at that time, I would have responded that they were policemen in plain clothes. We kept eating and talking about the project. We avoided saying anything about the elections or about what was happening in the square. It was getting late, and the driver of our car came in to tell me that we should be leaving as soon as possible to make sure we get to Sarande before dark. He was concerned, he explained, that the police could stop us on the way, take his license away, and tell me that the car was not fit to continue. We stood up right away, said our goodbyes, and left. We made it to Sarande; early the next morning, we left for the beautiful island of Corfu.

The situation in Albania turned to the worse. The most dramatic development was the failure of the pyramid-scheme companies. These companies lured investors in their direction by promising quick and high returns, sometimes up to 50 percent. Hoping for a dramatic increase of their savings, Albanians invested whatever money they had. Some of them sold even their belongings, home, and real estate to increase their investments and get rich quickly. Warnings by international financial institutions against the pyramid schemes were ignored, and the government did nothing to stop or control them. In fact, the rumors were that even high-level government officials were involved in them. By the latter part of 1996, the pyramid schemes stopped attracting new investors and one after the other stopped making payments. In the meantime, most of them took out of the country the millions of dollars they had amassed.

Realizing that they were losing their savings, the people were devastated and started protesting. The government reacted by arresting the leaders of the pyramid schemes and seizing whatever funds they still held in Albania. During that period, one of the project team leaders was at the University of Washington working with us under a Fulbright grant. She stopped by my office and expressed serious concern about her father. After losing all his savings and being deprived of any income, he became extremely depressed; he withdrew to his room and would not talk to anyone. How sad, I thought, that people who had suffered so much for so many years had to go through this, just as they thought things were looking up for them.

Things escalated to an armed revolt throughout the country that could not be contained by the armed forces. "On March 9," Biberaj wrote, "Berisha reached an agreement with ten political parties, which provided for a national reconciliation government, general amnesty for rebels, the surrender of arms within a week, and parliamentary elections in June 1997."[6] The unrest continued and foreigners left the country for security reasons. With a request by Berisha for international intervention and the consent of the United Nations, a multinational force was sent to Albania by the end of March. They restored reasonable calm in the country, and on June 29 new elections were conducted in which the Socialist Party prevailed, Sali Berisha resigned as president less than a month later, and a new era began for Albania.

As a result of what happened between the elections of May 26, 1996, and those of June 29, 1997, the UW project came to a stop in about February 1997 and we were on a waiting mode. We were also disappointed with what took place. As I reported to our funding agency in August 1997, "the last several months made it obvious that Albania has not yet been able to achieve a transformation to a democratic society."[7] At the same time, we were determined to move forward. My determination was strengthened by Milika Dhamo, one of the team leaders and, at that time, a UW visiting Fulbright scholar. In view of the turmoil in Albania, she could have asked for asylum in the United States. She was living with her family in an elderly lady's home who offered to donate the entire house to her if she decided to stay. Milika was highly tempted, but she refused. As a Fulbright scholar, she had agreed to go back. She could not disappoint those who trusted her. In addition, she felt that she had an important role to play in the democratization of Albania. This was evident to Milika now more than ever before the most recent events in her country.

5

Publishing the Materials and Starting a Network

Publishing the Manual and the Teacher's Guides

The 1997 events created a very difficult situation for us. There was less safety around the country and the economic conditions were poor. With the establishment of a new government in Tirana, new leadership emerged in the Ministry of Education. We were not sure how they would react to what we had done thus far and planned to do in the near future. In the meantime, we were faced with a number of delays in our activities. As a result, we had to keep getting extensions on existing grants so that we could complete the related activities. At the same time, we were applying, as well as receiving, new grants for additional activities. It sounds complicated, and it was, but with patience and hard work, we were able to move forward and achieve our objectives.

Thus far, we had manuscripts for teacher's guides ready for publication for grades one through seven, including those developed by the Albanian Educational Development Project (AEDP) for grades one through three. We also completed a manuscript for the manual on democratic citizenship education, but we were requested to consider doing some additional work on this document. In view of what had happened since the elections of 1996, our funding agency recommended that we add a chapter on the threats to democracy. We considered this to be a worthwhile recommendation and decided to do it. Before publishing these documents, however, we wanted to develop manuscripts for teacher's guides for grades eight through ten. The production and publication of all of these materials were necessary before embarking on an ambitious plan to train thousands of teachers on how to use them properly.

Although a number of Albanian educators were working in developing and finalizing the teacher's guides, the leadership team was working on identifying the threats of democracy. To do so, they searched the literature and carefully studied the Albanian situation. A number of questions were raised. What caused the 1992 optimism toward the democratization of Albania to fade away? Why the reversal? Where should the blame fall for what happened in Albania and for the suffering inflicted on the Albanian people? The leadership team went all the way back to the ancient teacher *Isocrates* to identify six enemies of democracy as follows: "factionalism, excessive individualism, poverty, overpopulation, corruption, and despair."[1] In addition, the leadership team used a quote from former Secretary General of the United Nations, Kofi Annan, to point to the causes for the failure of democracy: "Where there is insufficient accountability of leaders, lack of transparency in regimes, inadequate checks and balances, non-adherence to the rule of law, absence of peaceful means to change or replace leadership, or lack of respect for human rights, political control becomes excessively important and the stakes become excessively high."[2]

The Albanian scholars chose to become more direct and more specific in identifying the causes for the reversal in the newly established Albanian democracy. They attributed the failures to the following key factors:

- lack of democratic tradition,
- authoritarianism and unlimited power,
- people feeling that their vote was violated,
- lack of conflict resolution skills,
- lack of transparency in government,
- lack of infrastructure, and
- lack of a viable economic system.[3]

With a sense of disappointment, the leadership team concluded that "these threats have been and continue to be present in Albania, and they are threatening the development of the democratic system."[4] This realization shook their confidence to the point where, for the first time, they questioned the potential of the project contributing toward the democratization of Albania. "Can the schools," they asked, "develop a new generation of citizens that would be willing and capable to work toward the elimination of threats?"[5] In view of the situation, the expression of doubt was justified, but fortunately, it did not last very long. Moving forward with the younger generation was deemed easier than trying to change the old generation. The older people grew up under a different system and most likely would not be able to succeed regardless of their rhetoric favoring democracy. They have a hard time giving up authoritarian tendencies. The new chapter that resulted from this research and discussion, entitled "The Major Threats of Democracy and the Albanian Experience," was incorporated in the manuscript as the third chapter of the manual, which was now ready for publication.

The manuscripts for the teacher's guides for grades nine and ten were developed by Drs. Milika Dhamo and Marjana Sinani in partnership with two other Albanian scholars familiar with the textbook content in each of the two grades. Unfortunately, the teacher's guide for grade eight was not developed as the corresponding textbook for that grade on economics was not approved by the special committee of the Ministry of Education. As pointed out in a previous chapter, this is traditionally a common practice in the Balkans. School textbooks are considered to be the instruments for developing or sustaining national identity and must be closely monitored by the authorities.

The manual on democratic citizenship education and the nine completed teacher's guides were finally published in 1997 in cooperation with the AEDP project of the Soros Foundation. Nineteen thousand copies of the manual were printed in the Albanian language. We wanted to make this document available, not only to as many teachers as possible, but also to school administrators, government officials, and politicians. One thousand copies of the manual were made available in the English language for anyone from abroad having no knowledge of the Albanian language. The teacher's guide for each grade, excluding the eighth grade, was made available in 2,000 copies for a total of 18,000 copies—one for each social/civic education teacher in the country. The printing was done under the direction of Mr. Barthul Musai of the AEDP in cooperation with the core leadership team. The cost for printing all these materials was $120,000, half of which was paid by the Soros Foundation. Under these conditions, we had no problem allowing the AEDP to add its logo on each publication.

The published materials were the instruments through which the teachers would promote the ideas of democracy to their students and lead them toward the development of democratic ways. To accomplish this, the teachers themselves had to commit to democracy, especially the values of freedom and service to the common good. But would they be able to do it? We had to raise this question among ourselves because we were aware of the conditions under which the teachers lived during the fifty years of the communist regime. They have not experienced freedom, and their human dignity was constantly violated. They were forced to work for the system without adequate rewards for themselves and their families. Whatever was left of their time at the end of the day, they were compelled to devote it to a struggle for their own survival and that of their loved ones. Standing in line for hours to get bread or other food items, for example, was very time consuming. Living that way, they felt like they were closed in a cage, and they were too tired to think for themselves. At the same time, they were not allowed to exercise their own personal initiative.

We hoped the materials would be adequate to get the teachers out of that cage, taste the rewards of freedom, and start thinking beyond their narrow interests. One is not free until she or he can widen her or his horizon and show concern for others and the common good. We felt strongly, however, that this would not happen by just handing over the materials to the teachers. Teachers would need to be instructed on how to use the published materials properly. We decided, therefore, to pursue a new phase in the project—the training of the teachers. The more teachers we trained the easier and more effective it would be to prepare the new generation of Albanians for democratic citizenship.

Introducing the TTT Model and the Training of Teacher Trainers

The Training of the Teacher Trainers (TTT) model was adopted for the training of the teachers. It was a model developed during the late 1960s and early 1970s by a cluster of more than thirty projects throughout the United States, including one at the University of Washington. All projects were funded by the then U.S. Office of Education. The project at the University of Washington was under the direction of Professors John Jarolimek of the College of

Education and Phillip Bacon of the Department of Geography. I was fortunate enough to be invited from New York to be the third person to play a part in the project's operation and academic activities. The main objective of the TTT projects was to respond to the realization that the social studies curriculum and the methodology for teaching it were outdated.[6] Both the curriculum and the methodology needed to be changed. The best way to do it would be through the training of the teachers.

The social studies curriculum in the United States had been designed in 1916 and remained the same throughout the years. The content was organized on the basis of what came to be known as the *expanding horizons* approach. The students would start in the early grades learning about their families and communities. They would then expand their study to the region, state, nation, and the world. With drastic developments in transportation and communication, however, the horizon of the students expanded in their real-world experience, especially in the elementary school, while the corresponding social studies content remained the same. As a result, children and youth continued to learn things they already knew or whose significance was minimized by the rapidity of developments. My doctoral dissertation in the early 1960s contributed to this realization.[7] I discovered, for example, that children in the third grade in school did not need to study the arrangement of the grocery store, as they did when the grocery store had first emerged. The private car had made it possible for them to visit the grocery store at least once a week since early childhood, so they already knew how the groceries were arranged or where to find various items.

In addition, teaching methods were confined to memory learning, thus depriving the students from developing the ability to understand situations and social phenomena. Not enough attention was given to the development of intellectual skills and the ability for self-directed learning. As mentioned earlier, a properly educated citizen in a democracy should be able to analyze social situations and issues, consider alternative solutions to problems, and have the wisdom to select solutions upon which to act on the basis of what will benefit the greatest number of people.

In view of this situation, the need for change in the curriculum, as well as the methodology of social studies education, was evident. Consequently, the content of social studies in the schools was streamlined to correspond with developments in the fields of social sciences. As early as the mid 1950s, the National Council for the Social Studies (NCSS) published new themes for the social studies program.[8] At the same time, the intellectual skills, and later the consideration of issues, were included in the teaching of social studies. Now teachers had to be instructed on how to incorporate these changes in their professional work, and the TTT projects made this possible. Hundreds of college and university professors were trained on the new content and methods of teaching. They, in turn, introduced the new developments to thousands of new as well as in-service teachers throughout the country. Some of the major leaders in social studies education in the United States during the last forty years were TTT graduates, including several of them from the University of Washington.

With the vivid memory of the successes of the TTT project, I did not hesitate to propose to my Albanian leadership team that we use the same approach in Albania. We agreed that such an initiative would be the best way to begin the establishment of a countrywide network capable of introducing democracy to the country. Instead of college and university professors, however, we selected five of the best teachers from each of the thirty-seven school districts in the country to be trained as teacher trainers.

By this time, securing funds for our activities became easier. Impressed with our production of teaching materials, our cooperation with the AEDP, and our vision to establish a network for teaching democracy throughout the country, the United States Information Agency (USIA) placed the University of Washington Civic Education Project (UW project) in Albania on a sole source basis. Every year, they would ask us to estimate how much money we needed for the following year. They would then reserve that amount until we formally submitted a proposal. I felt quite honored with the level of confidence demonstrated toward the University of Washington and me personally. I once called the head of the USIA unit overseeing our project to ask for funding for a particular activity. His response was, "Professor, you did so much with a relatively small amount of money; how can we refuse you?" This was a most rewarding response. It was moments such as this that kept me going during difficult times.

By midyear in 1999, we were ready to begin the training of the teacher trainers. However, the Socialist government was in power and the situation was not yet settled. This forced us to make some modifications to our proposed activities. The original plan was to take 4 American educators to Albania during March 1999 to join the leadership team for the training of more than 185 prospective teacher trainers. Unfortunately, the Americans were not allowed at that time to travel to Albania due to prevailing unsafe conditions in the country. Instead, we decided to have the Pedagogical Research Institute of Tirana to conduct the three-day-long training in cooperation with the AEDP. Dr. Sinani, a key employee of the institute and one of the leaders in our project, and Dr. Barthul Musai of the AEDP were selected to lead the effort. Other members included in the training team were Drs. Dhamo of the University of Tirana and Fatmira Myteberi of the Pedagogical Institute—both were members of the UW project leadership team.

As a result of the safety problem, the funding agency approved our request to amend the contract and have the four designated members of the training team fly to Seattle and work with us in preparation for the training workshops. The expenses for this trip were jointly covered by the UW project and the Soros Foundation project. A request had also been approved for a later meeting with the training team somewhere in Europe. The conditions in Albania improved sufficiently, however, and it was not necessary for this later meeting to be moved outside the country. The workshops took place in five different universities as follows:

- University of Shkodra—September 23–25, 1999;
- University of Elbasan—September 27–29, 1999;
- University of Gjirokastra—October 4–6, 1999;
- University of Korca—October 11–13, 1999; and
- University of Tirana—October 16–18, 1999.

The program was organized in such a way that the participants had never before experienced. Teaching methodologies and techniques resembled those recommended in the preceding chapter. Instead of just listening to lectures, the participants were involved in the learning process by interacting with the instructors and among themselves. The objective was not to simply deliver information to the participants, but also to challenge them to explore the meaning of concepts, analyze situations and traditional practices, evaluate social principles and beliefs, propose solutions to social problems, and learn the skills necessary to lead a life that is guided by reason and a concern for the common good. And they should do all that within a peaceful context and with respect for each other.

To achieve these goals, the presentations on the basics of democracy and democratic citizenship education were short. They were followed by discussions during which the participants were encouraged to raise questions. In some cases, the participants were divided into small groups to discuss a particular presentation. The discussion was led by an instructor or by one of the participants. After a set time, the participants would reconvene as a whole in order for each small group to report on their discussion. Each participant had been provided with a copy of the manual on democratic citizenship education in Albania, and they were encouraged to read it with a critical mind. Opportunities were then provided for them to seek clarifications and raise questions in private or in front of the entire group.

A considerable amount of time during each workshop was devoted to interactive teaching through demonstrations. All participants were asked to choose a lesson from the teacher's guide of their own grade and study it carefully. Then, they were instructed to select a concept or a skill from that lesson and prepare to teach it to their peers by interacting with them. This approach is known in the educational literature as *peer-teaching*, and it is used extensively in elementary schools, high schools, and even in higher education. The trainer is always there to intervene through questions, if necessary, to change the direction of the discussion. The trainer can also intervene, if needed, to make sure the discussion is done in an orderly manner and is not monopolized by a limited number of learners.

Time was allowed at the end for each workshop to be evaluated on the basis of a number of questions prepared in advance. Included among the questions prepared by the training team were the following:

- Did the workshop enable you to understand the concepts of democracy, civil society, and active citizenship?
- Did you see any advantages in the interactive model of teaching?
- What is your impression of the program of the workshop?
- Do you think the workshop prepared you to teach other teachers?

The teachers overwhelmingly appreciated the openness, as well as the disciplined nature, of the presentations, demonstrations, and discussions. Though 17 percent of them questioned their ability to teach the interactive methodology to others, they all found it useful as well as exciting, and they were willing to give it a try. All participants expressed a desire for additional seminars of this nature, but more importantly, they recommended workshops of this type for all social studies and civic education teachers. All participants were awarded certificates as teacher trainers that were specially designed and jointly issued by the Ministry of Education and the University of Washington. These certificates were received with considerable enthusiasm.

PREPARING MATERIALS FOR PRE-SERVICE TEACHER EDUCATION

It did not take us very long to realize that university students preparing to become social studies teachers, and eventually civic education teachers, needed special training on democracy while they were still at the university. They needed to know the basics of democracy and democratic citizenship education. More than that, they needed to develop a commitment to democratic ideas and processes. We felt confident that the universities would respond positively to any recommendations we made toward that purpose. As pointed out earlier in this book, the faculty of the University of Tirana opened its doors to me for the delivery of a lecture on democracy in 1991, when the communists were still in power. The University of Elbasan did the same during the early stages of the UW project. Five universities around the country offered their facilities to be used for the five initial workshops on open and interactive teaching.

A good example of the desire of the members of university faculties to become active in the democratization of the country was Professor Bekim Como's actions following his trip to the United States. A professor at the University of Tirana, he was one of two faculty members to visit the University of Washington in 1992. Upon his return to Albania, he sent me a very warm letter expressing his profound appreciation for his experience in the United States. More importantly, and with the approval of the Ministry of Education, he proceeded right away to bring about change in

Albania. As he stated in his letter, "I have assumed a new task for myself, and with the help of my colleagues and students, I will move forward." Within a short period, he organized a student group to discuss and promote democratic ideas and causes. The name of the group was *Education under Democracy.* I was thrilled to participate in the second meeting of the organization where the students presented papers on various aspects of democracy. It was obvious that they had taken their assignments seriously. More importantly, they demonstrated a passion for democracy and pointed to its benefits for the Albanian society. Professor Como's vision was filled with ambition to institutionalize the deliberate teaching of democracy. As he concluded in his letter, "we are constantly feeling a greater need to enter into further branches of university pedagogy with the initiation of a course on the theme of Democratic Civic Education."[9]

It was decided, therefore, to start experimenting with the development of two textbooks for university students preparing to become social studies teachers. One of these books would be for those preparing to teach in elementary school, and the second book would be for those preparing to teach in secondary school. Funding was secured for two Albanian professors to come to the University of Washington to prepare for the task. Professors Adem Tamo and Yuli Pango of the University of Tirana were selected for this particular innovation. They arrived in Seattle on November 13, 1998, and returned to Albania on December 2, 1998.

Before embarking on this task, we met to define its scope and specify the various responsibilities for the authors, along with the process for fulfilling those responsibilities. After considering several alternatives, the following agreement was articulated as a reminder and was signed by all three of us:

- Dr. Tamo agreed to develop the manuscript for the book to be used by students preparing to teach elementary school;
- Dr. Pango agreed to develop the manuscript for the book to be used by students preparing to teach secondary school;
- The manuscripts would be in the Albanian language, but each author agreed to prepare a summary translation in English no less in size than one-fifth of the full manuscript in Albanian;

- The manuscripts and their translation would be sent to the University of Washington for review as soon as it is completed, but not later than August 31, 1999;
- Following the review, feedback would be sent back to the authors for their consideration; and
- The authors would work with the AEDP staff to publish the books.

While the Albanian professors were in the United States, they were first teamed up with American professors who were specialists in the same fields to explore social studies and civic education. The Albanian professors developed the following titles and chapter headings for each book:

Civic Education for Democracy in Elementary School
Social studies and the elementary school
Developing instructional objectives in elementary social studies
The curriculum of social studies in the elementary school
Teaching and learning strategies in social studies at the elementary school
Critical issues in Albanian social studies teaching and learning
Assessing the student learning in elementary social studies

Civic Education for Democracy in Secondary School
Introduction: The basis and essence of social studies
Objectives of social studies for future secondary school teachers
What should secondary school students be taught?
The dimensions of social studies: social, psychological, developmental, and universal—those applying to all disciplines and subjects taught in school
How should secondary school students be taught?
The assessment of student achievement
Conclusions

A review of the details in the outlines revealed the authors' understanding of social studies education as taught in the United States and the Western world in general. They appeared to have a grasp of the qualities a democratic citizen should have as well as the methodologies that should be used to develop these qualities in pre-university students. The authors fully agreed with the content as well as the methodologies of democratic citizenship education as presented throughout this book. It should also be mentioned that Professors Tamo and Pango took some time during their visit to attend the annual meeting of the NCSS. They witnessed the proceedings of the meeting and explored new social studies and civic education books as well as other types of curriculum materials on display during the meeting. This experience helped them to reinforce some of the notions that had been expressed in the chapters of their pending book.

The manuscripts were developed in Albania on time. The summaries provided by the professors in the English language revealed a well-written expansion of the outlines. There was no need to interfere with what these two gentlemen were recommending for Albania. The project paid for the publication of one thousand copies of each book with the understanding that they would be made available to the students free of charge. More on the distribution of the books will be presented in a later chapter dealing with the development of civic education centers in the universities.

CULTIVATING WIDER FIELDS AND SEEDING DEMOCRACY'S IDEAS AND WAYS

Although the project was preparing curriculum materials and trainers for in-service and pre-service civic education teachers, other opportunities were also pursued to assist in the promotion of democracy. A number of nongovernmental organizations (NGOs) had emerged in the country wanting to help the country come out of its worst dictatorship; we raised a number of questions to guide us. Could they play a role in our democratization effort? How about the various international organizations and governments coming to the well-intentioned rescue of Albania? Could they be drawn in to help us in achieving some of our objectives? Was there a way to motivate the media to be more deliberate in supporting the democratization process? How about the politicians and the various government officials, could they be brought closer to our democratization efforts? We initiated the following activities in response to these questions.

Connecting with NGOs: As alluded to above, following the break away from Communist rule, Albanians were encouraged to form NGOs to promote various democratic causes. Included among these causes were *human rights, civil rights, women's rights, gender equality, children's rights,* and many more. The overall goal of these organizations has been and continues to be the promotion of civil society by encouraging citizens to assist in three basic ways: to get along with each other, to show an interest in fulfilling their responsibility in influencing politicians and government officials to serve the common good, and to take responsibility for directly contributing to the common good through voluntary and independent civic engagement. The focus of each NGO is narrow, but when all of them are considered together, they constitute a significant force in pressuring elected officials to work for the benefit of the people. NGOs are funded by a variety of sources, but most of them get their financial support from outside the country.

As a European Commission report pointed out, the government of Albania accepted the role of NGOs. At the same time, however, the European Commission reported that "Albania would benefit from a government policy which more actively encouraged the involvement of NGOs in the decision making process."[10] We had noticed the potential of the NGOs since the early stages of the UW project. We decided, therefore, to recruit them as occasional partners in our democratization effort. Since they had the government's approval and their causes were compatible with democracy, we felt that we could benefit from their energy and commitment. We invited them to operate their programs within the context of our constantly expanding network. A number of NGOs welcomed the invitation because our project gave them access to educators throughout the country.

Attracting the International Organizations: Most often the international organizations function like an NGO. They are interested in promoting democracy, but they usually address one particular aspect of democracy, and they have a limited amount of time and resources to achieve their objective. Often, they would come in Albania with a broad objective and had no idea of how to proceed. Our project had the people, or the contacts, to help them finalize an activity and carry it out using our network.

Attracting the Mass Media: The mass media at the local as well as the international levels showed an interest in what we were doing.

They would show up at various workshops or other events, tape scenes of interest to them, and show them in the evening news. Reports related to the project were also published in newspapers, including *Mesues* (The Teacher), a newspaper published by the Ministry of Education. I had a basic speech on democracy that I was using in part or in its entirety as I was traveling around the country. This speech was translated in the Albanian language. Reporters would ask for a copy and often used extensive parts from it in their reports.

In addition to these activities, the team responsible for the training of the teacher trainers provided another opportunity for the media to publicize the project. They decided to videotape selected training workshops to use them later for instructional purposes. Several of them were analyzed later during the teacher training workshops. Some videos were made available to the media and were shown to the general public. The overall idea was to bring democracy to the attention of as many people as possible and make them partners in our efforts to democratize the country. If democracy was to be advanced in Albania, the people had to join in and play their part. It was their responsibility to control and guide the government officials, and this media exposure helped increase their awareness and desire to move in that direction.

Organizing a National Conference on Democratic Citizenship Education: Politicians and government officials are very important in the democratization process. During the transitional period of the late 1990s, most of the democratization attempts were undertaken from the top down mainly with the involvement of politicians and government officials. As it will be elaborated later, those attempts were not as successful as expected. We feel that democratization can have better results when approached from the bottom up. Even in this approach, however, the role of the politicians and government leaders is very important. They are the gatekeepers and nothing can be achieved without their approval and cooperation. That is why our project stayed in constant communication with them and never proceeded to the next stage without first informing them and obtaining their permission. But we wondered how we could reach more of them and bring them closer to what we were doing?

To that end, we organized a national conference on democratic citizenship education. In order for the conference to be successful, the approval and attendance of the minister of education was a priority. Early in June, Dr. Sinani met with Minister Athem Ruka and received, as she reported, his "enthusiastic support." She also brought to his attention a suggestion to invite to the conference a limited number of academics and educational leaders from the neighboring countries to the North. The minister appreciated that suggestion and recommended that the conference take place at the beginning of the 1999–2000 school year. It actually took place on October 28 and 29, 1999.

Labeled as the *Conference on Democratic Citizenship Education*, it was planned by the project's leadership team under the guidance of Dr. Barthyl Musai of the AEDP. Since the conference was not in our original plans, the AEDP offered to cover the expenses for the event. The participants came from throughout the country and included most of the two hundred teachers who were trained as teacher trainers. Other local-level educators were also included. The minister of education was there, along with many members of the parliament and high-level government officials. A few individuals from neighboring countries also participated in the event. Following a limited number of brief speeches, the main part of the program consisted of presentations by the teacher trainers on their training experiences and the effect the training had on their teaching.

It should be noted that all the public media were present during the conference and their reports publicized its proceedings widely. Those present were most impressed by the presentations of the teacher trainers—their enthusiasm for what they had experienced and their passion for democracy. The teachers felt privileged counting themselves among those playing a part in the democratization of their country. Did the conference make a difference? It certainly did. More people had the opportunity to participate in or witness the demonstration of democratic ways. More people joined the expanding network, and by doing so, increased the potential for democracy becoming a reality. This is critical, because the people are the foundation of democracy. This is clearly implied in President Abraham Lincoln's well-known description of democracy as "government of the people, by the people, for the people."

6

Expanding the Network and Addressing Feedback

Coping with Troubling Bureaucratic Delays

With the exception of the teacher's guide for the eighth grade, all curriculum materials needed for the civic education teachers' training were completed. The teacher trainers from school districts around the country were instructed on how to use the materials, and they were ready to play their role as instructors for their colleagues. The funding for the civic education teachers' training was also in place, including almost half of the amount needed coming from the Albanian Educational Development Project (AEDP). In the meantime, the new socialist government that was elected in 1997 had assumed full power. It was functioning as well as it could be expected under the circumstances. The higher officials of the Ministry of Education were replaced with Mr. Ethem Ruka as the minister of education and science. One of the project team leaders, Dr. Marjana Sinani, happened to know the minister personally. She made an appointment and met him to inform about the project and let him know that I was planning on writing to him.

On November 4, 1997, I sent a letter to Minister Ruka outlining the project's activities and achievements thus far. I also asked for his cooperation, as well as his permission, to continue with the project. Two weeks later, I was very pleased to receive the following letter, dated November 18, 1997. In this letter, which was labeled as *LETTER OF SUPPORT*, he said the following in his own words:

> Dear Prof. Kaltsounis,
>
> It is my pleasure to write to you and your university. I highly appreciate your engagement and that of the University of Washington in the Project on Democratic Citizenship Education in Albania.
>
> We hold that citizenship education is essential to the preservation and improvement of the democratic society and to its governance. In order for the children to grow effective citizens, school needs to provide them both with a common body of knowledge and a realm of intellectual and participatory skills. I hope this project to help Albanian schools, teachers and students reaching reasonable standards in civic education.
>
> Looking forward to further cooperation with the University of Washington.
>
> Sincerely,
>
> (Signed and sealed with the ministry's official seal)
>
> Athem Ruga[1]

The letter was exactly what we needed to continue with the project. The minister could not have articulated his support in a better and clearer way. Consequently, the work started and the years 1998 and 1999 went by without any problems. All curriculum materials were published as planned. As already mentioned, the only problem we faced was some delay in the development of the teacher's guide for grade eight. It could not be done because the Ministry of Education had not yet approved the textbook for that grade, so we decided to wait. Meanwhile, the workshops for the teacher trainers were successfully carried out under the leadership of Dr. Sinani, representing the Pedagogical Research Institute, and Dr. Barthyl Musai, representing the AEDP. The activities for the two years were completed with a very successful national conference on democratic citizenship education that has already been covered in the previous chapter.

As the year 2000 was approaching, we were ready to begin the training of all civic education teachers throughout the country. The training team would consist of the teacher trainers, now available in each district, under the direction of Drs. Sinani and Musai. A detailed budget was already developed and a schedule was drafted calling for the training to be completed by the end of June 2000. The project's core leadership team was enthusiastically looking forward to the task, especially after a short visit in Tirana by Madeleine Albright, the secretary of the U.S. Department of State. Madam Secretary met with the team members, listened to a brief report on their activities, congratulated them for their successes, and encouraged them to continue. The vice minister assigned to oversee the project was already preparing a letter for the districts to inform them that teacher training on civic education was about to start.

Unfortunately, things did not work out as planned. Situations emerged within the partnerships involved that caused the project to experience serious and unproductive delays. If it was not for the patience of the University of Washington, the understanding of the U.S. Department of State, and the high level of commitment on the part of the Albanian core team, the project would most likely have collapsed. Convinced that the difficulties could be overcome, we decided to be patient as developments were unfolding. From an operational point of view, the partners in the project consisted of the Albanian leadership team of the University of Washington (UW) project, the funding agency, the University of Washington, the Albanian Ministry of Education, the Pedagogical Research Institute of Tirana, and the Soros Foundation's AEDP. All of these entities had to play their part according to the plan in order for the teacher training to be carried out successfully.

The first indications of a problem came from the AEDP. Initially, approximately half of the funds needed for the teacher training were to come from the AEDP. We were aware that the AEDP was going through a drastic reorganization, but we had no idea that this reorganization was going to adversely affect our plans for training the teachers. The reorganization was completed early in June 2000. Soon after that, the newly appointed director, Mr. Vasilaq Zoto, informed us that the promised financial contribution by the AEDP for the teacher training would not be possible. We had to come up with a solution to this problem. Fortunately, the AEDP's earlier contribution for printing the curriculum materials made it possible for our project to save $75,022.00, so this amount was still available at the University of Washington. Permission was sought and obtained from the funding agency to add that amount to the funds that have already been allocated to the University of Washington for the training of the teachers. It should be mentioned here, parenthetically, that the United States Information

Agency (USIA), our funding agency, was consolidated within the U.S. Department of State, so from that point onward the funds for the project were coming directly from that source.

The situation at the Ministry of Education was getting complicated. We were approaching the end of June, and we still had no specific permission to train the teachers. By this time, the task of overseeing the UW project was turned over to one of the vice ministers, Mr. Andrea Marto, and two other ministry officials, the director of the Project Monitoring Unit, Mr. Ilia Paluka, and the director of the Pedagogical Research Institute, Mr. Bujar Basha. During the second half of July, I received a letter signed by all three of these officials. A copy of the letter was sent to Mr. Zoto, the newly appointed director of the AEDP. The letter appeared to express support for the teacher training, but at the same time, it revealed a desire on their part "to institutionalize," as they put it, the training of the teachers activity. To accomplish this, they requested that I submit to them an "official proposal" composed, as they stated, of (1) major objectives, (2) main beneficiaries, (3) planned activities, (4) overall budget and its detailed distribution, and (5) main indicators for assessment of the project. They closed the letter by justifying these requests on the basis of a May 18, 2000, Ministry of Education regulation on the procedures for "Submission, Approval, and Follow-up of Projects in the Educational System."

I responded to that letter with one of my own dated July 22, 2000. So that they know where I stood, the first paragraph of this letter read as follows:

> The Civic Education Project in Albania that I have the privilege of directing has been going on since the early nineties. It is the opinion of many observers and interested parties that this project made significant progress in advancing democratic citizenship education in Albania. It did so, in my view, because it had the support of three Ministers of Education, three Vice Ministers, three Directors of the Pedagogical Research Institute, and many Albanian educators who deserve most of the credit for whatever was accomplished. In directing this project, my basic principles were: (a) not to impose anything, but to expose Albanian educators to democratic citizenship education and assist them to adopt whatever they thought was appropriate for Albania; (b) not to write any of the curriculum materials myself, but to assist Albanian educators, selected and sent

to me by the authorities in Albania, to do the writing; and (c) to keep informing the authorities and asking for their consent on whatever we were doing.

Then, I pointed out to them that everything was done on the basis of proposals to the U.S. government, which always had been shared with the Albanian authorities. The proposals would not have been approved by the U.S. Department of State without the written consent of the Albanian Ministry of Education. Though I considered their request for a proposal superfluous and in some ways perplexing, I went ahead and expanded on the items of their suggested outline, including the budget. I did this with the hope that such a gesture would encourage them to consent for the teacher training.

The next official response from Albania arrived as an e-mail message in October 2000. It was sent by the director of projects but it was signed by the vice minister, with a copy again to the director of the AEDP, Mr. Zoto. The message started with an expression of their readiness, including that of the Pedagogical Research Institute, to start the teacher training. The message then concluded with this statement: "Now we have only one problem: we need a more detailed budget."[2] They already had a list of the general categories of the budget, including the amounts allocated for each category, but they were asking for more details. No justification was provided for such a request.

There were compelling reasons for me, however, to remain in control of the budget. Every dollar in the budget was tied to the specific expenditures that had been outlined in my proposal to the U.S. government. The process for distributing the funds was also set. My proposal was submitted to the U.S. Government in my capacity as a faculty member at the University of Washington. The funds were awarded not to me personally but to the university, with me designated as the custodian. This meant that I was the only one who would request distribution of funds. The university was obligated, however, to make sure the funds were distributed to me on the basis of the specific provisions of the proposal. A signed receipt was also required for each item of expenditure. If funds were used for any purpose or item other than those specified in the proposal, I was personally accountable for them. Under these circumstances, it was not possible for me to turn the budget over to someone else. It was necessary that I have absolute control of the finances.

During the period these communications were exchanged, the project's Albanian core leadership team was in constant communication with the three ministry of education officials assigned to the project. They always faithfully reported to me about the meetings. As the reports were accumulating, I saw a pattern developing. One report was positive while the next one was disappointing. Quite often, my coworkers would be excited after having been told that they had approval to start the training, but the excitement did not last long. During the next meeting, they would be stopped from going ahead on the basis of some excuse or no excuse at all. Was this a delaying tactic?

Puzzled by the situation, I reviewed all the messages to see if I could discover any particular concerns expressed by the Albanian authorities, other than the budget. One such concern was articulated in one of the messages, which noted that "the project is not a project of the Institute." How could that be possible when the institute was a part of the project from its beginning? The director of the institute was among the officials of the Albanian Ministry of Education who had traveled to Seattle as a participant in the project's first activity. Many of the ideas for the UW project came out of discussions in which members of the institute were heavily involved. Two members of the core leadership team were members of the institute appointed by the Ministry of Education to come to the United States for a two-month training period. The same people were involved in writing the teacher's guides. Other members of the institute were also involved in the writing of the teacher's guides for the first three grades under the cooperative agreement between the AEDP and the UW project. The training of the teacher trainers was based in the institute and was coordinated by Drs. Sinani and Fatmira Myteberi, both of them members of the institute. Previous directors of the institute stayed close to the project and cooperated with us in a number of ways. Given all these facts, I could not understand why these three gentlemen would make such a statement.

Another concern implied in the letter from Messrs. Marto, Paluka, and Basha was a desire on their part to move the teacher training from "a small number of specialists (the group you've worked with so far,") as they stated, "into a national network."

Unfortunately their assessment of the project at this point was also wrong. Expanding the network was one of our primary objectives ever since the UW project started seven years earlier. By July 2000, the group with which I was working comprised well more than two hundred people. All of these people were Albanian and well trained as teacher trainers. The three ministry of education officials insisted on bringing in new people to train the teachers, even though we had no assurances that these people had any training on or experience in a well-developed democracy. We argued strongly that the training of civics teachers had to be done by Albanian scholars/educators who were well trained for the task.

As reported through one of the messages, the leadership group was asked at one point to submit its lectures to the Ministry of Education and the Pedagogical Research Institute before getting permission for the training. That was unfortunate. Censorship and democracy do not go together. The team members refused to do so, and I was very proud of them for refusing. Their response to this incident was one of the strongest indications for me that democracy was going to eventually be consolidated in Albania.

The situation was becoming rather frustrating, to say the least. I could not help but ask myself the following questions: Why is this happening? Why would the Minister of Education approve the continuation of the project and then allow his people to place roadblocks? What is it exactly that bothers them? Why are they not open with me? Did we do something during the last seven years of our involvement in Albania that violated their trust in us? Why are they hinting about involving trainers who were not specifically prepared for the task? What else can we do to move the project forward? Despite these questions, we were determined to wait. We have gone too far to stop at this point. There was so much to be done, and the Albanian people deserved it.

INVOLVING THE U.S. DEPARTMENT OF STATE AND THE AMERICAN EMBASSY

Perplexed and disappointed as I was, I decided to bring these difficulties to the attention of my main contact person in the U.S. Department of State, Dr. Marie Westbrook, and ask for her assistance. She chose to discuss the matter with the Cultural Officer of the American Embassy in Tirana, Ms. Deborah Jones, and ask for her advice. She also suggested that I write to Ms. Jones, giving her as much background as possible and identifying the issues for her. Giving the background was easy, but identifying the issues was difficult. I urged Ms. Jones to try to preserve the integrity of the training by first seeing to it that it would be based on what was already achieved. Second, I emphasized to her that the teacher training should be carried out by those Albanian scholars and educators who had already been trained as trainers. I reminded her that those same people also wrote the training curriculum materials. I also pointed out that it would be difficult at this point to have other Albanians step in to conduct the teacher training. By this time, the year 2000 was over. Hoping for the matter to be resolved, we kept asking for no-cost extensions on three different overlapping contracts.

On January 12, 2001, Dr. Westbrook reported that Ms. Jones had "a very productive meeting in the Ministry of Education and anticipated no particular problems in continuing with the training of the teachers." Ms. Jones also met with the director of the institute separately and found him "to be open and cooperative as well." On the same day, I also spoke over the telephone with Ms. Jones who suggested, in addition, that I go to Albania soon to get things going. On that suggestion, I made arrangements to go to Tirana, arriving there on March 18, 2001. Dr. Westbrook also decided to be in Tirana during that same time, arriving there a day later.

Shortly after our arrival in Tirana, a meeting with all concerned was organized in the Ministry of Education. This meeting was attended by Minister Ruka, the American ambassador, vice minister Marto, Dr. Westbrook, the director of the institute, and members of the UW project's core team, including myself. Mr. Paluka was out of the country, we were told, and unable to attend. After a roundtable discussion, it was once again agreed to proceed with the teacher training as planned by the project. Minister Ruka issued another official letter of support that was addressed to me, with copies to the U.S. Embassy in Tirana and Ms. Deborah Jones. The letter read as follows: "Ministry of Education of Albania is indeed very grateful for the outcomes we had with the project on civics education in Albania. We express our continued support from the Ministry of Education in Albania to ensure that training of teachers on civic education project continues to move forward." It should be pointed out that Dr. Westbrook was outstanding in this discussion as well as others that followed. She was well informed about the project, direct, and most effective in her arguments.

After this meeting, one would think that the drama would have ended at this point, but unfortunately it did not. Before leaving Albania, I met with Mr. Basha at the Pedagogical Research Institute, and he still wanted to bring in fifteen new trainers. In order to win his support, I offered to accept his recommendation, provided we first trained the individuals he would recommend. With Mr. Basha agreeing to that, I asked the leadership team to prepare a plan and present it to Mr. Basha for training these fifteen new teacher trainers.

With everything seemingly in place for the teacher training, Dr. Westbrook and I decided to go to the Northern city of Shkodra. Dr. Westbrook wanted to meet with a group of professors at the University of Shkodra who were quite active in democratization activities. We left early in the morning with an Embassy car, which, I was surprised to find out, was an armored car. Shkodra was in the territory where the opposition was strong at that time, so outsiders had to be careful visiting. Following a long and productive meeting, our hosts wanted to show us their famous Shkodra hospitality and invited us to a restaurant for a late afternoon lunch. As the day was rapidly coming to an end, the driver advised us to leave so that we could be out of the area before it became dark. We made it, but the driving was quite fast.

The next day, we were on our way back to the United States. A few days later, I received a message from the team telling me that they had delivered the plan to Mr. Basha for training the fifteen new trainers. A few days later, Mr. Basha informed them that he was rejecting the plan as irrelevant to the institute. Not knowing what to do, the team took the plan to Mr. Paluka who found it acceptable and offered to bring the matter to the minister's attention. Informed about this, I decided to send a message to Mr. Paluka on May 31. After telling him that he was missed at the meeting in the ministry, I informed him about Mr. Basha's refusal to accept the plan for the training of the new trainers. At the same time, I asked for his intervention with Mr. Basha. On June 5, Mr. Paluka reported that after contacting Mr. Basha, he found him to be in full agreement with the plan as presented to him. After that, I was totally confused. I did not know who and what to believe.

While the negotiations were going on and we were in a waiting mode, a number of people in the Pedagogical Research Institute were fired early in July, due to a disagreement with their director. The firing created a considerable amount of tension within the Institute and attracted the attention of the media. About a week later, Dr. Sinani, an important member of the institute and the leader of the teacher training team, was also fired. This was devastating to Sinani, her family, and to all of us who valued and respected her. In the meantime, a national election was held in Albania in which the Socialist Party prevailed for another four-year term. This brought a change in our situation because the minister of education lost his seat in the parliament. Under these circumstances, we had to wait for a new team to emerge in the ministry. In addition to expecting a new minister, we were also anticipating new vice ministers and a new leader at the Pedagogical Research Institute. We were also hoping for the reinstatement of Dr. Sinani.

ACHIEVING THE TRAINING OF THE CIVIC EDUCATION TEACHERS

The changes we anticipated did materialize. Mr. Ben Blushi, a vibrant and outgoing younger man, became the minister of education and science. The new vice minister assigned to oversee our project was Mr. Sokol Axhemi. The director of the Pedagogical Research Institute was suspended for cause and Dr. Erlehta Mato, one of the authors of the teacher's guides for the first three grades, was later appointed to take his place. The most important appointment made by the new minister, for the project of course, was the rehiring of Dr. Sinani. Not only did he reinstate her, but he elevated her to the position of deputy director of the Pedagogical Research Institute. As we were approaching the end of 2001, everything looked bright for the project. We felt that it was worth the wait. On the other hand, we kept wondering: Did anyone gain anything from the delays? On the contrary, the hidden agendas and the lack of openness caused all of us to lose something, especially the Albanian people who, unlike some of their leaders, demonstrate a thirst for democracy and its benefits.

On November 4, 2001, I sent a long letter to Vice Minister Axhemi informing him about the UW project. In addition to the project's history and achievements thus far, I described in that letter the process of funding the project. I did this in order to make him aware of the restrictions imposed on me by the funding agency and the University of Washington. It was important for the vice minister to understand from the beginning the need for me to be in control of the budget. Then, I pointed out that the project worked for years without delays, except during the uprising of 1997 and the last two years. Concerning the latest delays, I wrote this to him, "What has been frustrating for me was the fact that I have never been able to find out what the reason was for the delays." The letter continued with a presentation of the plan for training the teachers. In closing, I asked for his support and permission to undertake the training of the civic education teachers as soon as possible. On December 5, 2001, I had a response from vice Minister Axhemi revealing full familiarity with the project's history and achievements. He expressed his satisfaction with the progress made thus far and announced the ministry's decision to have us proceed with the teacher training, as planned, and under the direction of Dr. Sinani. The project was again in a full-operational mode.

The plan called for sixteen workshops to take place in different locations around the country. The locations were in major cities easily accessible by the teachers in the surrounding villages. In preparation for the workshops, the following needed to be done in advance:

- Notify local education authorities about the workshops in each location and appoint a local person to coordinate logistics;
- Instruct the local coordinators on their responsibilities;
- Finalize the program for each workshop, including identifying the lecturers and preparing the materials to be distributed and used by the participants;
- Notify the teacher trainers in each district to prepare for their role in the workshops;
- Prepare budgets for each workshop closely reflecting the project's basic budget; and
- Establish a procedure, as well as the proper forms, for distributing the funds and securing receipts.

The project's core leadership team was ready to proceed with these preparations. There were four members in the team when it was originally established. We lost one member, Dr. Myteberi, who immigrated to the United States. It was a great loss for the project and for Albania. Another member, Dr. Tonin Gjuraj, took a demanding position as director of International Relations for the University of Shkodra, and he could not participate as much as he would have liked. He was very active, however, with the training of the teachers in the city of Shkodra. It is interesting to note, parenthetically, that Dr. Gjuraj is now serving as the Albanian Ambassador in Israel. All communications with the local educational authorities were done by Dr. Sinani in her capacity as the deputy director of the Pedagogical Research Institute. Dr. Sinani also joined Dr. Milika Dhamo in organizing the materials for the workshops, including sending sets of materials to the teacher trainers to assist them with their preparation. The two leaders were assisted by two persons temporarily hired for the duration of the workshops. The lecturers consisted of all those trained in the United States or those involved in the development and writing of the teacher's guides.

The budget for each workshop was prepared by Drs. Sinani and Dhamo. I reviewed every one of the items to make sure they did not exceed the overall amount allocated for the training of the teachers. I also made sure the proportions spent for each category in the budget reflected the proportions approved by the funding agency, which had a policy of holding down administrative expenses. As alluded to earlier in this book, the funds designated for the training of the teachers were wired to the Tirana Branch of the National Bank of Greece through its Branch in Ioannina, Greece, a city very close to the Albanian border. It was easier for me to do this since I spoke Greek and had no problem communicating with the bank's personnel. In view of restrictions imposed in the United States due to terrorism, I had to register the opening of the account in Tirana. This account was under my name and the names of Drs. Sinani and Dhamo.

The amount of money I could forward to the Tirana account at any particular time was relatively small—no more than $12,000. As far as withdrawals from the bank were concerned, two of the three authorized individuals were required to be at the bank to sign for each withdrawal. Since I was in Tirana only occasionally, Drs. Sinani and Dhamo did the withdrawals and forwarded the accounting to me for each workshop. It was embarrassing at times, but I had to be quite demanding on obtaining receipts for every dollar that was spent. Drs. Dhamo and Sinani did a great job getting the receipts and submitting them to me on time. The University of Washington would not advance an amount requested unless the accounting for the previously withdrawn amount was submitted and approved.

The training started in Tirana with a meeting for all logistics coordinators of the sixteen workshop locations. They spent one day in learning about the project and familiarizing themselves with what they were expected to do. Their responsibilities were to facilitate teachers with transportation and accommodation arrangements, especially those from the surrounding villages. They also saw to it that the rooms for the workshops were well prepared. In the large cities of Tirana, Elbasan, and Vlore, where the numbers of trainees were large, all instructors worked together. They also worked together during the workshop for the teachers of the Tirana suburbs. For the rest of the workshops, the instructors were divided into two groups and were conducting two workshops at the same time in two different locations.

Chronologically, the sixteen two-day workshops were scheduled in two rounds. The first round took place between June 29 and July 11, 2002, as follows:

- June 29–30: Sarande, including teachers from Delvine and Gjirokastra;
- June 29–30: Korca, including teachers from Devoll and Erseke;
- July 1–2: Elbasan, including teachers from Gramsh;
- July 6–7: Permeti, including teachers from Tepelene;
- July 6–7: Shkodra, including teachers from Malesia e Mathe and Puke;
- July 8–9: Durres, including teachers from Kavaja;
- July 8–9: Berat, including teachers from Kucove and Skrapar; and
- July 10–11: Tirana (suburbs).

The second round of workshops took place between August 24 and September 22, 2002, following this schedule:

- August 24–25: Vlore, including teachers from Fier;
- August 31–September 1: Tirana (city);

- September 7–8: Tropoje, including teachers from Has and Kukes;
- September 7–8: Lushnje, including teachers from Peqin and Malakaster;
- September 14–15: Peshkopi, including teachers from Bulqize;
- September 14–15: Mat, including teachers from Mirdite;
- September 21–22: Kruje, including teachers from Kurbin and Lezhe; and
- September 21–22: Pogradec, including teachers from Librazhd and Perrenjas.

Each workshop was scheduled to start at 8:30 in the morning and go on until 4:30 in the afternoon. The program was divided into two parts. Most of the first day was devoted to lectures and discussions on the basics of democracy and democratic citizenship education. The lectures reflected the basic democratic concepts, values, and skills contained in the manual, *Democratic Citizenship Education in Albania*, which was distributed to all teachers in advance. The lecturers also elaborated on strategies and techniques that encourage students to interact with the teacher and between each other. Following the lectures, the participants were given enough time to select a lesson plan from one of the teacher's guides and shape it for implementation the following day during peer-teaching sessions. The second day was dedicated mainly to teaching the prepared lessons to their peers. This was done under the direction of their colleagues who had been trained earlier as teacher trainers. At the end of each day, the teachers were asked to evaluate the activities of the workshop.

A review of the written evaluations revealed that the teachers approved of the way the workshops were conducted. They especially enjoyed the independent activities as well as the group work. As one teacher wrote, "In this seminar, I found as most worthwhile the communication and collaboration among the participants." They wished they had more time devoted to reworking lesson plans from the teacher's guides. They also wanted more discussion on the lessons taught to their peers. Asked about changes they anticipated in their teaching as a result of the workshop, one teacher expected to "allow her students to raise more questions." Another teacher would "change the evaluation methods for the pupils and do more work in groups during the teaching hour." "As a result of this experience," another teacher wrote, "I have a better ability to communicate with my pupils." The teachers also found more meaning in their work. "After this training," one teacher wrote, "I will feel more responsible in my duty for the education of the new generation." As Professor Dhamo noted in one of her messages during the workshops, "The feedback from the teachers was wonderful."

The training of the teachers was finally completed. Based on the feedback from the teachers and the excitement observed during the workshops, it was a unique achievement. The democratic citizenship network was now expanded from a small group of scholars and educators in the early 1990s to an army of more than three thousand democracy builders. Located in just about every community in Albania, they will teach the younger generation to think and act democratically. They will work from within to help consolidate democracy in Albania.

TRAINING GREEK MINORITY TEACHERS AND RESPONDING TO FEEDBACK

There were no plans to separately train the Greek-speaking teachers in the Greek minority schools of Southern Albania. This idea came from the leadership team after they discovered there was some money left over from the training of the civic education teachers. The money was saved due to overestimating the cost of each workshop. When the proposal was submitted to the U.S. government in 1999, we asked for funds to train 3,000 teachers. Due to the delays, however, the cost per workshop went up. As a result, we asked in 2002 for permission to lower the number of trainees to 2,750 teachers in order to be able to stay within the allocated budget. But this time the cost was overestimated by approximately $5,000.00. The leadership team asked for permission to use that money for training the teachers in the Greek minority schools.

When the team leaders brought the idea to my attention, I asked them about the objectives of the proposed workshop. They informed me that the objectives would be to help teachers understand democracy, develop their inclination and ability to engage in open teaching, and apply the interactive approach to teaching and learning. I had no problem with that, and neither did the funding agency. The concern expressed by the leadership team for the teachers in the Greek minority schools was commended and appreciated. As reported to me later, the workshop went well. The language used was Albanian, but during the group discussions, the teachers were encouraged to use, if they so wished, their own language to communicate among themselves. It is worth mentioning that the Member of Parliament from the minority area, Dr. Vangelj Tavo, attended the workshop. He was impressed with it to the point where he paid for all teachers to go to the nearby Greek island of Corfu for a weekend.

Finally, after so many unnecessary bureaucratic delays, the training of 2,750 teachers in the implementation of interactive teaching was completed. A network of approximately 3,000 teachers/educators was now in place enthusiastically teaching democracy and putting democratic ways into practice. This was especially true at this point with the 200 teachers who had been trained as teacher trainers earlier. They had more time in the implementation phase and had gained more confidence. The activities recommended in the teacher's guides were very helpful, but the teachers were encouraged to go beyond these activities and develop their own activities, as well. The members of the leadership team were monitoring this inspiring dimension of the project with a considerable amount of satisfaction. They decided to ask the teachers to write down the new activities they developed, as well as any other comments, and send everything to them. What was received was very useful feedback.

Impressed by the new activities and the comments provided by the teachers, all authors of the teacher's guides decided to revise them and produce a second edition for each and every grade, except, of course, for the eighth grade teacher's guide, which, as explained earlier, was not yet available. The manual on democratic citizenship education was also revised and enriched by Drs. Sinani and Dhamo. The U.S. Department of State was kind enough to eventually provide the funds for the printing of the revised materials. They were available for distribution to the schools in 2004.

The network was established, but how could we make sure it would survive and continue to be active? Our attention was now turned to finding a response to this important question.

7

Network Strengthening through the Universities

Turning to the Creativity, Energy, and Power of the Universities

The bureaucratic delays described in chapter 6 made things difficult for us but we did not give up. We felt proud of what we have achieved, and we were committed to our vision. We were held up for a while, but we were determined to sail forward and take our ship to its destination. As far as we were concerned, the democratization of Albania was inevitable and could not be stopped. Convinced that the teacher training would eventually take place, we begun looking for ways to go beyond that point. Just establishing the network was not enough. We had to find a way to sustain and nourish the network, as well as guide it in its work. Our initial plan was to turn the network over to the Ministry of Education and terminate the project. However, we were convinced that the Ministry of Education was too busy to assume another responsibility of enormous proportions. The demands of a highly centralized educational system would have made it impossible for the Ministry of Education to give democratization the attention it deserved. On the other hand, we felt strongly that we should stay within the educational system. After all, we were trying to bring about change through the younger generation now in school. Could the universities step in and assume a leading role in sustaining and advancing the democratization movement?

As pointed out in chapter 5, we had noticed an interest on the part of the faculties in certain Albanian universities to play a role in the democratization process. Two members of the project's leadership team were directly connected professionally with the university system. While still waiting for permission to conduct the teacher training, the leadership team explored the idea with university authorities, including Dr. Eduart Andoni, vice minister of education in charge of higher education. The idea was also pursued with the funding agency. The universities, as well as the U.S. Department of State, were receptive to the idea. The universities were quite excited at the prospect of joining the democratization process of their country. The project presented them with an opportunity to step outside the box of simply following directives from a centralized authority, and instead use their creativity to try something new. Encouraged by the high level of interest, we proceeded with the development of a concrete plan to have the universities assume a key role in the advancement of democracy in Albania.

Since the emerging democratization network consisted mainly of teachers and other types of educators from throughout the country, the leadership team determined that the universities selected for participation must have a teacher education program. There were five such universities in Albania located in just about every region of the country: the University of Shkodra, the University of Tirana, the University of Elbasan, the University of Korca, and the University of Gjirokastra. It was our ambition to include all five of them in the civic education program. The plan called for the establishment of a *Center for Democratic Citizenship Education*[1] in each one of them. Each center would serve as the intellectual hub on democratization for the university and the surrounding region. It would organize and carry out in-service workshops for each region's teachers as well as plan and manage democratization activities at the local level. Furthermore, each center would intensify efforts to prepare new teachers in the area of democratic citizenship education. At the same time, it was expected that the centers would introduce the teaching of democracy to each university's entire student population.

As early as 2001, long before the completion of the massive training of civic education teachers, a proposal was submitted to the U.S. Department of State requesting funds to make it possible for the University of Washington (UW) project to carry out the following activities:

- Secure space for the center in each university and equip it with appropriate furniture, a telephone, a computer, and other basic instructional equipment;

- Purchase and place in each center as many publications as possible on democracy and democratic citizenship education available in the English as well as in the Albanian language;
- Train two professors from each university on democracy and democratic citizenship education with an emphasis on implementing the curriculum materials developed and published by the project; and
- Arrange for each center to organize and carry out a workshop for in-service social studies/civic education teachers in the area under the supervision of the project's leadership team.

The development of the five centers was expected to take at least two years. It would also require more money than was available during the first year. As a result, the scope of the 2001 proposal was limited to the following two objectives: (1) to develop the democratic citizenship education center at the University of Tirana, in the capital of Albania; and (2) to train the professors from all five universities, which would take place in Tirana, while the center was being established at that university. The training of the professors, including the workshop for the in-service teachers of the city of Tirana, was scheduled to take place either in December 2001 or in March 2002. We were hoping that by that time the pending training of the teachers throughout Albania would have been completed. Unfortunately, however, this did not happen. As it turned out, the massive training of the teachers took place during the second half of 2002. As a result of the delay, we could not yet establish the university centers, because it would have made no sense to do so until the teachers' training was completed.

With clear indications that the training of the teachers would take place during the second part of 2002, we decided to revise the initial proposal for the development of the civic education centers in two ways. First, instead of starting with the development of the center at the University of Tirana, we decided to add a touch of decentralization in the process by starting with the four regional universities. We were encouraged to go in that direction by the American Embassy, which felt at that time that the development of the countryside needed more attention. The second change was to modify the management team of each university center by structuring it as a partnership between the university and the schools in the surrounding area.

To make these two changes possible, additional funds were requested to simultaneously begin developing the civic education centers in all four of the regional universities. The center in Tirana would be the last one to be established during the next funding cycle. To cast these centers in the mode of partnerships, the personnel of each center would be increased by adding six teachers from the surrounding area to the two professors. The teachers would be carefully selected, mainly from among those already trained by the project as teacher trainers. As a result of these changes, we decided to train the two professors and the six teachers of each university area together and at their own location. It was expected that this feature would establish a strong connection between the universities and their local educational system—a development that would enhance the centers' potential in the process of democracy building.

The second half of 2002 turned out to be one of the most productive periods of the project. Thanks to the overwhelming support of Minister Luan Memushi and Vice Minister Sokol Axhemi, the training of 2,750 teachers was finally completed. The U.S. Department of State approved our request to amend the scope and plan of our 2001 proposal for the development of the civic education centers. More funds were allocated for that purpose, and we were ready to move forward. It should be emphasized at this point that my role in carrying out the project's various activities was constantly diminishing. My Albanian coworkers, knowledgeable and capable, were doing most of the work in the field. They were especially skillful in attracting and engaging more people in the democratization effort. I was there simply to assist them in the development of proposals, to secure funds, and to make sure that the various proposals and budgets were implemented as approved. If changes on approved plans were found necessary, I would always be there to follow due process and make those changes possible.

With the recommended changes approved and an amended proposal in place, the four regional democratic civic education centers were developed within the time frame proposed. The first center at the University of Shkodra in the country's most northern part was established during the winter of 2003. The second center was developed in the spring of 2003 at the University of Gjirokastra in the country's southern region. The centers at the University of

Elbasan and the University of Korca were established at the same time, but separately, during the latter part of June and early July of the same year. As mentioned earlier, the democratic civic education center at the University of Tirana was established later, during the last part of January and the early part of February 2004 with funds provided for that year.

SETTING UP THE CENTERS AND TRAINING THE MANAGEMENT TEAMS

According to the plan, each university was asked to and did provide a room to serve as the democratic civic education center. Equipment such as tables, chairs, bookcases, and a telephone were also provided by the university. To make sure the universities were not overburdened accommodating the centers, \$3,200 was allocated by the project to each one of them to use as they saw fit. In some cases, a portion of that amount of money was used, for example, to temporarily facilitate the release of the two faculty members from other duties to participate in managing the center. An additional amount of \$2,000 was allocated directly to each center to purchase whatever instructional equipment they needed to facilitate its work, including projecting devices and a computer. In addition, any expenses for teachers coming from out of town were covered by the project.

The most important element of each center was its library. We prepared a list of books and other publications on democracy and democratic citizenship education that were available in the Albanian language. A number of basic books in the field that were available in English were also purchased and placed in the center's library. The UW project provided \$6,500 to each center to purchase as many of the publications as possible. It did not take long for the centers to become very attractive places. Each one of them was eventually decorated beautifully with meaningful displays reflecting the value of democracy. A sign was placed on the door and students would notice the centers and inquire about them. As soon as the teachers in the area were introduced to the centers, they found them useful, and they were delighted to visit them and spend some time in the stimulating environment of the university.

The program for training the two professors and six teachers in each center was similar to the program used for the training of the teacher trainers. It included the following features:

- Teaching the basics of democracy and democratic citizenship education, as presented in the manual, *Democratic Citizenship Education in Albania*;
- Presenting the interactive approach to teaching in order to introduce it to those not yet exposed to it or to reinforce it for those already familiar with it;
- Familiarizing the participants with the basic publications developed by the project during previous grant activity;
- Offering participants the opportunities to practice developing new lesson plans or revising existing ones from the teacher's guides; and
- Offering participants the opportunity to teach their lesson plans to their peers using the interactive approach.

In addition to following this overall plan, the workshop instructors addressed specific topics and issues brought to their attention by the participants. As reported by one of the project team leaders, these topics or issues included the following: dealing with the concept of change in personal as well as professional dimensions, group-work skills, needs assessment skills, managing democratic changes in schools, involving the school infrastructure and the community in democratic participation activities, writing proposals, and networking.

One way in which the training of the centers' management teams was different from that of the teacher trainers was the length of the workshops. The teacher training workshops lasted three days, while the training of the management team members lasted a full week. These groups needed to spend more time together to have more opportunities to practice teaching and discussing the concepts and processes of democracy. It was important for them to have the time to engage into a deep analysis of their peer-teaching so that they could see the value of the active involvement of the learners in the teaching and learning process. We also wanted them to realize the importance of teaching by example. The participants were encouraged to talk less and demonstrate more on how to involve students in their own learning. As emphasized elsewhere in this book, students should not be expected to learn everything from the teacher; they can also learn from each other and by themselves.

The final feature of the training was the staging of a workshop for forty-five in-service teachers from the surrounding area under the guidance and supervision of their trainers. The purpose for this workshop was to provide an opportunity for each center's team to apply what they themselves had learned. As in previous training sessions, the program for this workshop consisted again of two parts. The first part was to present and discuss the basics of democracy and democratic citizenship education. The second part was to adapt lessons from the teacher's guides and teach them to their peers. After each lesson was taught, a discussion took place to evaluate the lesson and determine ways in which it could be improved. One of the main criteria for the evaluation of each lesson was the extent to which the learners were involved in the teaching and learning process. Another criterion was the inclination on the part of those teaching to go beyond knowledge objectives and include the development of democratic values and skills. Did those teaching pay attention to the classroom environment as shaped by the behavior of those in the role of the students? Were they listening to each other courteously? Were they respectful of each other's opinions? Did they address effectively interfering negative elements in the classroom environment?

As pointed out earlier in this chapter, the training of the management team of the center of the University of Tirana was done later, but in a somewhat different way. The same was true of the entire process for establishing the Tirana center, which took place early in 2004. After discussions with Professor Ylli Pango, the then Dean of the Department of Social Sciences, the center for democratic citizenship education was, in a way, merged with an existing social sciences center. The latter was directed by Dr. Zana Sota, who joined the dean in welcoming the vitality promised by the mission and objectives of democratic citizenship education. It was agreed that Dr. Milika Dhamo, one of the most active leaders of the UW project, would be added as co-director to the newly formed center.

As with the other four centers for democratic citizenship education, literature materials on democracy and democratic citizenship education were added to the center. Since Dr. Dhamo and several other professors in the university were already trained, less time was needed for peer-teaching sessions. As a result, the decision was made to reduce the duration of the workshop to two days and concentrate on the training of the six teachers selected from the city of Tirana and the surrounding area. Another reason for reducing the length of the workshop was the close proximity of the University of Tirana to the Pedagogical Research Institute. Dr. Marjana Sinani and several other members of the institute were well trained and would be available to assist the Tirana center with their workshops.

Recognizing the Impressive Impact of the Centers

What was the impact of the centers for democratic citizenship education? Based on reports from the field sent by the leadership team, the excitement generated by the four centers already in place was attracting a considerable amount of attention. On February 28, 2003, Vice Minister Sokol Axhemi and Mr. Brian Shott, the Assistant Public Affairs Officer of the U.S. Embassy, visited the democratic citizenship education center at the University of Shkodra. They were joined by Ms. Mirela Cupi, assistant to the director of the Public Affairs Office of the Embassy; the director of education for the District of Shkodra; and the rector of the University of Shkodra. The eight members of the center outlined the nature of the center and its short-range as well as long-range plans. Working with the European Council, Dr. Dhamo spoke about her work within the context of the Stability Pact for the region. In connection with that involvement, she came in contact with the Education Development Center, Inc. (EDC). As Dr. Dhamo revealed, this worldwide organization was impressed by her presentation on the multiplier effect of the Training of the Teacher Trainers (TTT) model used in Albania for the training of democracy builders. As a result, the EDC was ready to send representatives to the Albanian democratic citizenship education centers to learn more about their work, with a special emphasis on the application of the TTT model.

In March 2003, the rector of the University of Shkodra met with the center's management team and spoke about his optimism for the center's potential to contribute toward the improvement of society. As Dr. Dhamo again reported, it was announced during that meeting that an application had already been submitted by the center to take part in a project on human rights and law empowerment sponsored by the United Nations Development Program. The center had also made arrangements to join *Call for Peace*, a project sponsored by an organization from the Netherlands to promote conflict resolution in the northwest section of Albania. The center's management team was also looking forward to working with *Education for Democracy*, an entity of the Council of Europe working toward stabilizing the area.

On April 11, 2003, Dr. Dhamo reported that an agreement was reached between the leadership team and representatives of *Human Rights and International Education*, a UNESCO project, to jointly train the members of the Shkodra and Gjrokastra centers on the human rights of minorities. Both of these cities and their surrounding area contain sizable numbers of minority people—Roma in Shkodra and Greeks in Gjirokastra. In addition, the center at the University of Gjirokastra organized a meeting with many key people to promote democratic citizenship education in early childhood education. Those participating in that meeting were two vice ministers and the rectors of both universities; Dr. Vangjel Tavo, a Member of Parliament from the district of Gjirokastra; all sixteen members of the centers of Gjirokastra and Shkodra, and Drs. Sinani and Dhamo of the UW project's leadership team. Though the centers at the universities of Elbasan and Korca were not yet completely developed, the rectors from both these universities were also invited.

On July 2, 2003, the University of Elbasan center held a workshop on technology and democratic citizenship education. Two representatives from each one of the four centers were trained on how to navigate the Internet for materials related to democratic citizenship education. The workshop was conducted by a New York University computer science graduate and an expert from the Council of Europe, assisted by Drs. Sinani and Dhamo, as well as by their assistant, Ms. Anila Sultarova. One of the outcomes of this activity was the development of Web pages in the participating centers. It should be noted that the University of Shkodra center had already developed its own Web page—the only one at the university.

The University of Korca center was working with the schools in the city to establish student governments. Later in October, the faith-based education specialist of the U.S. Embassy, Mr. Shefqet Shyti, visited the center to learn about the effort and observe student governments in action. He was escorted to three different schools. According to Dr. Dhamo's report, one school in a very poor and diverse area had its citizenship day. Sixteen classes were organizing activities on children's rights. In the other schools the student governments were planning other activities. Parents and teachers as well as the local educational authorities were present. Media representatives were also there recording the activities. "It was so impressive," Dr. Dhamo concluded, "to see one student government planning on having a new toilet in school, another talking about the rights of the physically handicapped and planning assistance activities for two blind neighbors." The student government of the third school was organizing a campaign with the motto *Let's Keep Our Korca Clean*. Mr. Shyti was very impressed. He took the team members to meet the American-educated Metropolitan John[2] of the Orthodox Church in Korca. Together they discussed ways in which the church and the schools could work together for the benefit of society.

By late October 2003, all four of the established centers reported the introduction of new courses in their universities on democracy and democratic citizenship education. In the meantime, arrangements with a number of international organizations were made to use the university centers as the avenue for training teachers on a number of democracy-related topics and objectives. These organizations originated from countries such as Austria, Switzerland, Norway, and Germany. In addition to human rights, the following topics were included: migration, anti-trafficking issues, and women's rights. It should also be noted that the centers demonstrated enough autonomy in their work to be themselves recognized and registered as nongovernmental organizations.

In closing this section, an article by Professor Ronald Gjini, a member of the center at the University of Elbasan, should be given some attention. In describing the center, Dr. Gjini reinforces the overall nature and activities of the centers thus far completed. However, the strong cooperation between the center and the Department of Social Sciences of the University of Elbasan does stand out. Through joint scholarly discussions, they strived together for a better understanding of democracy and the difference it can make in Albanian society. One of the main outcomes of working well together was the establishment in the university of a special program for the preparation of teachers in the field of democratic citizenship education—the first one in Albania.

The center reached out to the area's schools assisting them to initiate programs that would enable children and youth to develop into citizens willing and able to practice democracy. To accomplish this, the center instructed teachers as well as the students to practice democracy within their own school environment, such as working together harmoniously to keep their classroom neat and respecting each other. They guided them to examine their neighborhoods and communities to make sure people were not unfairly deprived of opportunities to pursue happiness. It did not take the students very long to realize, for example, that one segment of their community's population needing assistance was the abandoned children—a rather frequent practice in their country. Students then sought to cooperate with community leaders, including religious leaders, to look for solutions to the problem.

Professor Gjini concluded the article with this statement: "The experience accumulated this year through the activities of the center of democratic citizenship education has strengthened our belief that this center promises to continue being active into the future. We believe it will be an important instrument in promoting democratic citizenship education in the schools as well as the community. This belief is based on our qualifications and experience as well as the demonstrated cooperation with other institutions and organizations. We had and will continue to have the cooperation and support of the Social Sciences Department of the university, the regional education directories, the school principals, the teachers, the student governments, and the local NGOs."[3]

The Democratic Citizenship Education Centers Venturing on Their Own

Once the Center for Democratic Citizenship Education at the University of Tirana was established during the early part of February 2004, the network for the democratization of Albania through education was about to be completed. With the inclusion of the university system in the network, it was time to start thinking about ending the University of Washington's involvement. The Ministry of Education would be in a position to continue the democratization process under the leadership of the Pedagogical Research Institute. With the capable leadership at that time of Drs. Erlheta Mato and Sinani, the Pedagogical Research Institute was capable of undertaking the task. We were preparing, therefore, to turn the project over to the Ministry of Education with a national conference early in June, following an independent summative evaluation of the entire effort.

As we were preparing for the evaluation and the conference, we continued to be impressed by the centers' productivity. As a result, it was difficult for the leadership team to abruptly stop the project. Although keeping to our schedule as far as the final national conference was concerned, we decided to challenge all five of the centers by asking them to intensively pursue their own democratization projects at the local level. The U.S. Department of State agreed to provide a mini-grant of $10,000 to each center to facilitate this added phase, which was to be completed one year after the continuation of the democratization in Albania was turned over to the Ministry of Education. It is appropriate, I think, to pause at this point and close this chapter with a description of the process and the results of this added phase, before describing the evaluation and the final national conference in the next chapter.

The process was simple: We just asked the management teams of the five centers to come up with democratization projects at the local level. These projects would address one or more of the following: (1) bring the university, the schools, and the community together to work for the promotion of the common good of all people in their area; (2) train in-service as well as pre-service teachers on how to design and implement activities that would promote individual self-worth and responsibility; and (3) introduce democratic citizenship education as a field of study in the university, especially in teacher education. We urged the management teams to give as much emphasis as possible to projects that would involve cooperation between the university, the schools, and their community. The teams had to tailor their proposed projects within the limits of a budget, which could not exceed $10,000.

The proposals and the budgets had to be submitted for review by the core leadership team, including myself as the director of the overall project. This was done early in the summer of 2004.

The first set of proposals had shifted the emphasis from the local level to Tirana. The centers proposed to bring students from all over Albania to the capital for a series of meetings. This would have gone against the provisions of the proposal as approved by the funding agency, so the centers were asked to go back to the original notion and propose democratization projects that would take place locally. The teams responded immediately and the activities at the universities of Shkodra and Elbasan were completed by December 2004. The activities in Tirana were started late in December 2004 and were completed early in 2005. The activities in Korca and Gjirokastra were carried out during April, May, and part of June of the same year.

Upon completion of these various projects/activities, the five university centers were requested to prepare reports describing what they accomplished, and these five reports were compiled into a joint report by the core leadership team. In summary, this joint report described activities in the following areas:

- Teacher training activities at the local level;
- Youth activities on citizenship and civic action at the local level;
- Introduction of new courses on democratic citizenship education at the universities;
- Research on actual challenges for democratic citizenship education at the local level;
- Providing advice and resources on citizenship education; and
- Promoting cooperation between various ethnic and religious groups in the country.

Some of the projects and activities were quite interesting. For example, as reported by the team of the center at the University of Gjirokastra, a new course on democratic citizenship education was introduced to the second-year students of preschool and elementary-school teacher education programs at the Faculty of Educational Sciences. By decision of the University Senate, all university students were required to take the same course as of October 2005. A group of students from Asim Zeneli High School were guided by members of the center to organize and carry out a debate on civil rights and the right to vote. This was done in front of the cameras of local media, which broadcasted the debates to the public. The center also organized another activity at the Urani

Rumbo Elementary School in which seventy students participated, including a number of drop-out students. The medium of art was used to give the students an opportunity to express who they perceived themselves to be, and what needs and dreams they had as individuals. At the end, the students exhibited their artistic creations to be viewed by the students, parents, school officials, and a number of city officials. The objective of this activity was to build self-esteem and help drop-out students to return to school.

The student governments in the Stavri Themeli and Mesenjtorja e pare Shqipe schools in Korca decided to organize an activity to raise money to purchase books for their school libraries. The activities started with less than 15 students and ended up with 120 students volunteering to participate, along with their parents. They prepared traditional food items for sale during their school fair. To attract more people to the food fair, the organizers asked parents to bring in traditional embroidery items that were exhibited and described to the approximately 700 visitors. The benefits of this activity went beyond raising money for books. The students learned how to work together for a common goal, and in so doing, they built better relationships among themselves. In addition, they developed a number of skills, such as organization and marketing skills. They also provided an opportunity for themselves and the public to learn something about the artistic nature of their culture. A better bond was also created between the schools and the community. This activity was fully covered by the media and was repeated in ten other schools in the city as well as in some of the villages.

The center at the University of Elbasan initiated a number of activities to connect the schools with the community. The objective was to identify common problems and do something about them that would lead toward resolution. The work of the schools in Elbasan with abandoned children was mentioned earlier, but a new project with senior citizens living in special homes was also impressive. High school students would visit these homes regularly and try to do what they could to help the residents meet some of their needs. These visits were especially instrumental in breaking the monotony and the loneliness of the people in those facilities.

The newest center at the University of Tirana undertook an ambitious project to enable students to understand the system of market economy and its basic principles of private initiative and free market. The project started with the involvement of one class of students, but the entire high school was soon involved. The students at the various grades were instructed to develop their own company with a logo and its own board of directors, who were elected by all those participating in a particular company. The students identified market needs and developed a program to find ways to address those needs. They then established shares that were sold to anyone interested to create capital. Shareholders were promised to share in the profits proportionately on the basis of the number of shares they purchased. Samples of products produced for sale by the established companies included the following: food items made by the students and their parents, CDs with specific music pieces requested by the clients, hair care services, and traditional handmade items. The students used fairs and other ways to sell their products. Each company managed to make enough money to pay dividends. But more importantly, students learned market economy in a way that will never be forgotten and a number of very important life skills such as discussion, organization, planning, setting rules, expediting matters, problem solving, and getting along with fellow students and others in the community and society.

The democratic citizenship education center at the University of Shkodra engaged not only in extensive training within the university and in the surrounding schools, but it also involved students in activities addressing the needs of the community. One such activity took place in the communities of Koplick and Malesia e Mathe. After a seminar on the importance of a clean community environment, the high school students in those communities picked up the garbage from the streets and whitewashed the trunks of the trees on both sides of the streets. They followed this with a campaign to inform the people in their community about ways in which they could keep their environment clean. The students approached businesses in their towns and raised money to make posters and fliers on cleanliness, which they posted or distributed throughout the community. On hearing about the action-oriented activities in Shkodra, the U.S. ambassador visited the center in January 2005. She spoke on the importance of the contribution the center was making toward the democratization of Albania and congratulated the members of the center for a job well done. In return, she was offered an honorary membership in the center.

The activities described in the preceding paragraphs took place several years ago, but a more recent message from Dr. Dhamo, dated September 12, 2009, indicates that "the centers are alive." She goes on to list numerous local, national, and international donors supporting activities in all five of the centers, including UNICEF, United Nations, and several countries. "The Council of Europe has helped the Shkodra center in training young voters," Dr. Dhamo wrote, while the "Elbasan center carried out community activities of young students helping the elderly. Korca has been active in a series of activities with Gypsy and Roma children and their parents."

Whether new or old, the centers' activities justify our decision to involve the universities and allow them to unleash their creativity. The Albanian universities convincingly demonstrate their ability and determination to assume a major role in the democratization of their country. They have the trust of the people and can respond to their aspirations. People ask for major changes, and there is no better agent to bring about change than the universities. Our work with the Albanian universities convinces us that they can inspire ordinary people to work for democracy. Governments are important, but as it will be demonstrated later in this book, it is almost impossible for a government to achieve consolidation of democracy without the active involvement of the people. After all, democracy is basically the people's business.

8

Evaluating and Concluding the Project

Distinguishing between Formative Evaluation and Summative Evaluation

The most frequent forms of evaluation, especially in the field of education, are *formative evaluation* and *summative evaluation.* Formative evaluation is what teachers use almost daily to determine whether a student, or a class of students, achieved a particular learning objective such as understanding of a concept or a relationship between two or more concepts, the development of a certain value, or the ability to apply a skill. Some objectives such as knowing the name of a country, for example, can be expected to be learned within a short period. A more complicated objective, on the other hand, like understanding democracy or a relationship between concepts would take longer time. The development of values and skills would also require more time. The teacher should be in a position to determine how long it will take for a particular objective to be achieved on the basis of his or her knowledge of the students. The teacher's consideration of the students' individual differences is very important in evaluation because, although all students can learn, some learn faster than others.

The purpose of formative evaluation is to facilitate instruction. By using teacher-made tests, closely examining the students' performance in their daily assignments, or through observation, the teacher will know how well the students are doing. If most of them did not achieve a particular objective, the teacher adjusts her/his teaching. It is not fair to always blame the students for not achieving a particular learning objective because the possibility is always there that the teacher might have failed to effectively reach the students. That is why it is important at times for teachers to adjust their instructional approaches rather than blame the students for not learning something that was taught to them. The teacher must also apply what the professionals refer to as *differentiated instruction.*[1] This implies that the teacher gets to know well each and every student so that he or she can be able to vary instruction, giving more attention to those requiring special assistance. Not all students learn something the same way or, as already mentioned, at the same pace. As the teacher engages in differentiated instruction, it is important to make sure that no students are offended by making them feel inadequate.

In contrast to formative evaluation, summative evaluation in education is an assessment of learning at the end of an extended period of instruction, such as a school year. It is usually done to assign grades and determine whether a student is ready to be advanced to a higher grade. At the high school or university levels, summative evaluation can be the final assessment at the completion of a course. It can be based on a test or a combination of tests and data from other sources, such as portfolios and accumulated observations during the instructional period. Sometimes, it is difficult to distinguish formative from summative evaluation. The Northwest Regional Educational Laboratory agrees that "there is no crisp dividing line between formative evaluation and summative evaluation."[2] For example, a midterm examination in a college course can be used in the determination of the final grade as well as for instructional adjustment.

In the Albanian democratization project, we conducted both formative and summative evaluations. We conducted formative evaluations while implementing the project to find out how well the objectives of the various activities were achieved. Based on the data or feedback we collected, we modified the implementation process to achieve better results. The project activities involved development of educational materials, training on the proper use of the materials, and the demonstration of democratization activities in the school as well as in the community. In the case of the educational materials, we collected feedback from the teachers and used it to improve those materials and produce new editions. When we trained the teachers, we asked them to fill out questionnaires after each session, and we improved future training sessions based on the teachers' responses. We sometimes made videotapes of training sessions that we analyzed and evaluated to identify effective practices as well as those needing improvement. Finally, in the case of student activities aimed toward implementation of democratic principles and practices, we collected data through observation and used them for instructional purposes.

Even though some of our evaluations during the implementation period could be considered to be summative evaluations, the independent evaluation we conducted at the end of the project was definitely our most significant summative evaluation.

Establishing an Independent Team and Conducting the Summative Evaluation

We selected three individuals with strong academic credentials to comprise the evaluation team: Professor Nathalie Gehrke of the University of Washington in Seattle, Washington, USA, specializing in curriculum and teacher education; Professor Rolf Grankvist of the University of Science and Technology in Trondhheim, Norway, specializing in history, social studies education, and teacher education; and Professor Edmond Rapti of the University of Tirana in Tirana, Albania, specializing in educational psychology. We selected a Northern European, an Albanian, as well as an American for the team to make sure the project was viewed from a broad perspective. All three of the members had no prior direct involvement with the University of Washington (UW) project, but they were aware of its existence. Also, Professors Gehrke and Grankvist had met each other in the past.

The team was provided with background information on the project, and they were asked to develop their own procedure for the evaluation. All expenses were covered for them to travel to Tirana and spend a week working together on the evaluation. They could also travel anywhere in Albania for data collection purposes. The core leadership team was always available to the evaluators to assist them in any way they could to carry out their task. The team arrived in Tirana on May 23, 2004, and spent the first couple of days preparing for their mission. They talked to a number of people, including the members of the core leadership team, and visited a couple of schools in the capital to observe students involved in democratization activities. This was followed by a visit to the Center for Democratic Citizenship Education at the University of Tirana. Then, the evaluation team visited the other four centers in

Shkodra, Elbasan, Korca, and Gjirokastra. In addition, they visited four schools—two secondary schools, one elementary school, and one special education school.

Based on their report, the evaluators easily substantiated the project's basic assumption that democratization must come from within. The evaluators were convinced that outsiders were there simply guiding the Albanians toward development of a democratic system rather than imposing one upon them. The Albanian educators were taught the theoretical aspects of democracy and were exposed to daily life democratic practices common in other countries, but they were the ones to decide if and what democratic principles and ways should be introduced to Albania. The evaluation's additional findings were intended to answer a number of questions raised by the evaluation team: Was there any evidence that democratic principles and practices were incorporated into the educational system, especially in teacher education? Did the centers for democratic citizenship education have the potential to contribute to the democratization effort in Albania? Was the project successful? Finally, the evaluators were also interested in finding out whether there were any lessons to be learned by other countries from the democratization effort in Albania.

Upon completion of their task, the evaluation team presented its findings at the Civic Education National Conference, which took place in Tirana on June 5, 2004. Soon after the conference, they also submitted a written report.

PRESENTING THE FINDINGS AND RECOMMENDATIONS OF THE EVALUATION TEAM

The evaluation team presented the findings in the form of strengths and concerns. There were fourteen strengths identified as follows:

- The involvement of the teachers as a majority in the management team of the centers for democratic citizenship education;
- The joining of university professors and school teachers in a common effort;
- The support of the university administration at each site;

- The connections with the Ministry of Education;
- The strong coordination by the core leadership team of the project;
- The links with nongovernmental organizations (NGOs);
- The links with other international organizations;
- Approaching democracy education at multiple levels (elementary, intermediate, secondary, and university pre-service teacher education);
- The visible progress in reaching schools and classrooms in all sites;
- Supporting continuing conversation among those of different religions;
- Seeing citizenship in relation to Europe and the world, instead of just Albania;
- Supporting a new atmosphere and conversation between ethnic groups.
- The program centers' collaborative development of theoretical as well as practical materials, and the improvement of these materials over time on the basis of the needs of Albanian education; and
- The center's changing role to include not only teacher training, but also coordination of democratization activities.[3]

We appreciated the team's recognition of these positive qualities of the project. We were, however, disappointed that the team did not single out for praising the idea of networking. By adopting the Training of the Teacher Trainers (TTT) model with its impressive multiplier effect, thousands of teachers were trained within a relatively short period. In addition, the network's continuation was assured through the continuous in-service education provided by the democratic citizenship education centers at the various universities throughout Albania.

The evaluation team also expressed eight specific concerns:

- Securing consistent funding for continuing the democratization effort in Albania;
- Burn-out (exhaustion) potential for participants at all levels of the project;
- Limited planning for the long term with no visible plan documented;

- Somewhat uneven development of democratic decision and action processes at the site team level;
- Unevenness in the understanding of democracy among individuals in the sites, which could subsequently affect how the site participants could continue to deepen/enrich their theoretical and experiential understanding of democratic citizenship.
- Limited access to technology for communication among sites.
- Whether the centers could play a role of providing much-needed civics and pedagogy training for secondary teachers; and
- Ensuring that classroom democracy would not be interpreted as anarchy in which the teacher gives up all legitimate control as a democratic leader.

In view of the fact the evaluation took place as the project was closing, the unevenness of the understanding of democracy on the part of the teachers is understandable. Most of the teachers were trained late and relied only on their initial training. We hope that as the democratization continues, the democratic citizenship education centers will enhance the understanding of these teachers through workshops on a continuous basis. It should also be pointed out that the new civic education teachers will be prepared before they enter the teaching force, because just about all university teacher education programs developed courses on democratic citizenship.

In addition to identifying these strengths and concerns related to the project, the evaluation team articulated twelve recommendations:

- Plan continuing events and opportunities for deepening knowledge of democratic citizenship, for example, speakers, videos, teleconferences, texts, roundtable discussions, seminars, book groups, journals and monographs, especially for the trainers within the teams;
- Seek increasing ties and support within the Ministry of Education;
- Link the project's efforts to larger in-service and pre-service development efforts;
- Gather systematic data and evidence on teacher, headmaster, and school changes;
- Develop and implement training aimed specifically at local school board members, head masters of schools, and teacher inspectors;

- Continue to focus most heavily on development of teachers' knowledge and skills (civic teachers and teachers of other subjects) in (1) teaching academic content of democratic citizenship, (2) creating a democratic environment in the classroom and school, and (3) working democratically with partners in the project;
- Continue building a knowledge base about democratic citizenship education in Albania and share that knowledge among the center sites and the whole world;
- Support and study site variations in focus and capitalize on strengths of each site to share with others (cross-training);
- Encourage university professors to spend time in the schools: (1) working along with the teachers to experiment with new teaching strategies, (2) consulting and supporting teachers and headmasters, and (3) studying effects on the students and the school;
- Develop parent education programs on democratic citizenship education and on how to support teachers in their democratic citizenship education efforts;
- Experiment with teacher leaders co-teaching pre-service courses in democratic citizenship education with university professors on campus; and
- Develop a long-range plan for strengthening the cooperation between the centers through broad participation in planning.

The evaluation team made some very useful and far-reaching recommendations that take the democratization effort of Albania beyond the scope of the activities thus far implemented. Though some data were collected on changes noted in teachers and the school environment in general, it was done on an ad hoc basis or just through observation. As the evaluation team pointed out, an emphasis should be placed in the future on a more systematic effort to collect data. This systematic effort should be a well-structured attempt to collect data from the entire system, including the school environment, administrators, parents, as well as the students. In the case of parents, the evaluation team goes as far as to recommend implementing special democratization interventions with them. Our project did involve the parents, but only when the school activities called for them to participate, usually as observers. It is possible, however, that democratization activities aimed directly at the parents could speed up the democratization process. As explained in the next two chapters, I eventually recommend a new approach to democratization that places the parents and all ordinary citizens in a key role in the democratization process.

The evaluation team also recommended that the best and most experienced teachers should co-teach citizenship education courses to prospective teachers at the university. This is a sound recommendation that is consistent with our idea of including six of the best teachers in each of the five centers for democratic citizenship education. As it was pointed out earlier, one of the major activities of the centers was to introduce new courses on democratic citizenship for pre-service education teachers. The project even prepared textbooks for such courses.

Another worthwhile recommendation of the evaluation team was to develop a long-range plan for a joint effort by the five centers to continue the democratization of Albania. The recommendation for a plan is useful, but it can be argued that such a plan is inherent in the project's structure. The trained teachers will continue teaching democracy under the guidance of the centers for democratic citizenship education. The universities will continue to support the work of the centers under the leadership of the Pedagogical Research Institute—the appropriate arm of the Ministry of Education for the task. The institute is currently under the leadership of Erhleta Mato and Marjana Sinani, two individuals highly committed to the democratization process. This process is further enhanced by Albania's official decision to pursue the country's qualifications for admission to the European Union, including the establishment of a Ministry of Integration. It should also be argued that the new approach to democratization, which I address in more detail in chapters 9 and 10 is a plan for an effective democratization process, hopefully in the near future. This would not have emerged without the experience provided by the UW project.

The evaluation team's final recommendation was to continue advancing the knowledge about democracy and democratic citizenship education of all those participating in the democratization process. That has been the main focus of the project from the beginning. We started by developing the instructional materials for that purpose. We then taught democracy to teachers and trained them on how to teach in methods that will reflect democratic beliefs and practices. To continue deepening the understanding of democracy, we recruited the universities to continuously play a role in the process of democratization. There is no question that there will always be a need for a deeper understanding of democracy. Democratization is a process that has no end.

The evaluation team concluded the report with a number of positive general observations. The team praised the connection between theory and practice that the project was able to achieve. The fact that teachers and university professors were working together at the university centers, especially with the teachers in the majority, was recognized as a strong characteristic of the project. The evaluators also commented favorably about the *albanization* of the project's publications. Using feedback from the teachers, the project leadership team of Albanian scholars/educators produced revised editions to bring the publications closer to the reality of life in Albania. The evaluation team was also impressed by the comprehensive nature of the project.

As a last indication of the project's success, the evaluation team included this development in its report: "The University of Elbasan awarded to Theodore Kaltsounis the title of 'Professor of Honor' (Honorary Professorship) for his outstanding contribution in the democratization of the Albanian society through social studies teacher education." At the same time, and with the approval of the Ministry of Education, the center at the University of Elbasan was named "The Theodore Kaltsounis Center for Democratic Citizenship Education." These recognitions were most rewarding for me personally, because I had been struggling during the initial stages of the project for acceptance by the Albanians, while at the same time, I was dreaming for success that could lead to such recognitions.

Officially Concluding the Project and Looking toward the Future

During early June 2004, the centers for democratic citizenship education at the universities were still preparing to implement their democratization activities that were funded by the mini-grants. Those activities were scheduled to be completed within a year. Regardless, the decision was made to declare the overall project officially closed at that time and turn it over to the Ministry of Education with a national conference on civic education. After thirteen years with this project, it was time for the network of democracy builders that we produced to assume responsibility for its continuation.

The operational structure we put in place was very promising. Dr. Marjana Sinani of the Pedagogical Research Institute and Dr. Milika Dhamo of the University of Tirana were the undisputed leaders of the network. Dr. Sinani had recently been appointed director of in-service teacher education for the entire country. Their launching pad was the Pedagogical Research Institute under the leadership of Dr. Erhleta Mato, another committed champion of democratization. With the Ministry of Education's consent and their deep understanding of and commitment to democracy, they were ready to move forward. Working closely with the universities, they were capable of assuring the future productivity of the democratization network of thousands of teachers, students, and parents. They all wanted to realize the dream of a democratic Albania integrated with the rest of Europe to which Albania geographically belongs.

As for me personally, it was time for full retirement. This would afford me more time with my family, though I felt strongly that retirement would never imply a withdrawal from the challenges presented by the fields of education and democratization. These two endeavors have the power to inspire people to see beyond themselves and strive for something larger, more meaningful, and more fulfilling. I speak from experience. When I was growing up in Albania, I was struggling with two identities that had their roots in nationalism and were characterized by a spirit of confrontation. Getting away from Albania, and eventually from the Balkans, gave me the opportunity to see things from a broader perspective. My education and experiences convinced me to respect all people and act on the basis of logic and justice—what is reasonable and what is fair for all. I discovered that these principles form a mindset that is the foundation of democracy, and it is with this uplifting mindset that I came back to work in Albania. As I was withdrawing from active involvement, I had a strong feeling that we succeeded in leading young and old in Albania to think beyond themselves, respect others, and be guided in their lives by reason and fairness for all. With these thoughts in mind, it was time for me to move to the sidelines and enjoy following the developments.

It was appropriate, therefore, to close the project with a national conference that took place in Tirana on June 5, 2004. One hundred educators from throughout Albania were invited to participate, including all teachers and professors trained to operate the centers for democratic citizenship education at the various universities. The minister of education and the higher echelon of the Ministry of Education were also invited to participate, along with representatives from the American Embassy in Tirana. A few representatives from surrounding countries also participated in the conference, which was widely covered by the public media.

One of the main features of the conference was presentations by selected teachers on democratization activities in their school or the local community. The emphasis of the presentations was on the involvement of the students in the learning process. Also emphasized was the practice of democratic principles and processes by the students in their daily lives, both in school and away from school. The enthusiasm with which the teachers made their presentations was quite evident. They used visual aids to illustrate their activities, several of which were filmed by the media and were broadcasted throughout the country. Another main feature was a report by Professor Rolf Grankvist on the results of the summative evaluation. He was selected by the evaluation team to remain behind for a few more days to give the report. The tone of his presentation was most positive. He urged the authorities present to continue the project.

The final part of the conference consisted of three presentations. In my capacity as the director of the UW project, I outlined the project's achievements and recognized the Albanian scholars and educators who made it possible. More than anything else, I emphasized the belief that democracy cannot be transplanted; it has to come from within the country. I pointed out that we approached democratization through the educational system because we also believe that the best way to built democracy is from the bottom up—preparing the people for life in a democracy as early as possible in the process of democratization. On the other hand, I emphasized that the country's conditions cannot be ignored, nor can the government ignore its responsibility to improve those conditions. Finally, I called upon the government to continue the project by supporting the work of the leadership team and the entire network we put together.

Mr. Brian Shott of the American Embassy spoke on the importance of democracy as a way of life and expressed his satisfaction, and that of the Embassy, with the project's achievements. Finally, the minister of education of Albania spoke about the project's importance within the context of Albania's effort to democratize and integrate with the rest of Europe. He also expressed the ministry's commitment to assume full responsibility for continuing the project's activities.

Though the mini-grants were still in progress, the end of the conference marked the official end of the project—my active involvement in it at least. As I looked back at that point in time, I was able to identify a number of lessons learned: The first lesson stems from the diversity that is inherent in the democratization process. The involvement of many people and a number of institutions is required. As a result, differences of opinion do emerge and decisions are made that might not please all those concerned. So there is a need for *compromise*. Democratization is a dynamic process, and emerging conditions call for changes to be made in plans as you go. This situation calls for *patience*. One needs to stay focused not only on the overall objective, but also *open* to reasonable suggestions, if necessary, a situation that calls for *flexibility*. When the overall objective is threatened by unclear arguments and seemingly narrow interests, it is critical to *wait* for the right opportunity to move forward. *Do not give up*.

Another lesson has to do with the role of a country's leadership in the democratization process. Regardless of the approach used, it is difficult to move democratization forward without the *support of the country's leadership*. This is especially so when the democratization effort is done through the educational system. As the reader may recall, the project might not have even started without the support of the higher echelon of the Ministry of Education who visited the UW to learn about and experience democracy. They provided for us an atmosphere of acceptance within the ministry. Occasional roadblocks quite often tempted us to consider moving outside, but that thought was quickly rejected. We waited until the right person came along, mainly from within the system, to keep us on track. We also learned that whenever we have support from the country's leadership, democratization activities do advance at a faster pace.

We also learned that a country's democratization through education has to be approached *comprehensively* and with a *long-range plan*. Working only with a few schools, or just revising the curriculum without training teachers on how to use it, are not enough. Ways need to be found to involve the entire system and be prepared to work for a number of years to bring about meaningful and lasting change.

Finally, our belief that *democracy comes from within* has been reinforced by our experiences in Albania. Democracy puts the people in charge of their destiny. The government is there to serve the people and not the other way around. The people elect and control the leaders in power. In order to do that, the people need to be properly educated and skillful in the ways of democratic living. This is especially so in Albania where democracy is a relatively new experience and most of the current leaders grew up in one of the harshest dictatorships in the world. Our experience with the project convinced us that *democracy can be consolidated in Albania*, especially now that the European Union is seriously considering the country for admission. A way must be found, however, for the government and the people to join hands and work together for the consolidation of their democracy. This will lead to the Europeanization of the country. The indications are that Albania will succeed in meeting these objectives, but how long is it going to take? The next and final two chapters lead the way toward accelerating the democratization process so that the objectives can be achieved sooner rather than later.

9

Democratization and Albania's Experiment

Justifying the Need for Accelerating the Process of Democratization

The Albanian people made progress toward democratization, but there is no excuse for them to continue living in a country that is still classified as partly free. As mentioned in the introduction, those of us who worked hard for that country's democratization are delighted to observe improvements in local governance and the development of a civil society. However, we are disappointed that no significant progress has been made in other areas, especially national democratic governance, judiciary, and corruption. After almost twenty years since Albania rejected communist dictatorship, there is no reasonable justification for the slow pace of democratization. To counter this, the government needs to demonstrate more respect for the concerns and aspirations of the people. On the other hand, the people in general must develop an awareness of their rights and responsibilities in relationship to their government. They should vigorously, but peacefully, defend their rights and fulfill their responsibilities with zeal and determination. In other words, there is much left to be done in Albania before full democracy can be achieved.

In view of the situation, it was difficult for me to close this book having only described the University of Washington (UW) project. I felt the need to address the future of democratization in Albania and other countries around the globe in a similar situation. The progress in Albania thus far is important, but its effect could be quickly and seriously diminished without a plan to move forward toward consolidation of democracy. With this in mind, I added chapters 9 and 10 to provide a model for moving democratization faster beyond the electoral level. Though Albania is at the center of both these chapters, the goal is to look at the democratization process from a broad perspective and search for a new approach that can accelerate democratization anywhere. After a considerable amount of searching, such an approach emerged. It was derived from an analysis of existing models and the potential of the UW project to enrich and expand the democratization process.

While the new approach, or model, is presented in chapter 10, this chapter sets the foundation for it. More specifically, this chapter briefly discusses the *waves of democracy,* and their reverses, during the last two centuries. It also analyzes the various models of democratization and places the UW project in Albania within the context of the democratization literature. The contents of this chapter might be more appealing to democratization professionals, but it is also useful for anyone who wishes to understand the new approach and its practical implications.

THE THREE WAVES OF DEMOCRACY AND THEIR REVERSES

As Samuel Huntington informs us, the first wave of democracy in the United States of America started in 1828 with the expansion of voting rights to more males.[1] The stage for this movement was set earlier, of course, by the founding of the country and the establishment of its constitution in 1787. However, the majority of democratic reforms that resulted in a number of well-established democracies took place much later, during the early part of the twentieth century. There were two significant developments that prompted this first wave. The first was the crafting of the concept of *nation.* As quoted by Salvo Mastellone, the early nineteenth-century Italian revolutionary G. Mazzini, defined the nation as "the universality of citizens speaking the same language, associated, with equality of civil and patriotic rights, in the common purpose to develop and improve social forces and activities."[2] In other words, it is people with similar cultural characteristics desiring to live together in a well-defined territory, and they were willing to fight for it, if necessary.

The second development that propelled the first wave of democracy was World War I. It provided the opportunity for the nationalists of the time to realize their dream. The war dissolved existing European empires and replaced them with a number of small nations, most of them, especially in Western Europe, adopting a number of democratic qualities and institutions. At the same time, the Balkan peoples in Southeastern Europe started revolting against the Ottoman Empire. As a result, Yugoslavia, Bulgaria, and Albania were established as nations, though not under the banner of democracy. Greece, a neighbor of Albania, became a democracy during the second part of the nineteenth century, but World War I made it possible for her to practically triple her territory and expand democratic rule to the liberated Greeks inhabiting the newly acquired lands. Italy, another neighbor of Albania across the Adriatic, had become democratic just before the war started. Some thirty countries—mainly in Europe, but also in other continents—became democratic during the first wave of democracy that lasted until about a decade after the end of World War I.

Unfortunately, some of these newly formed democracies started reverting to autocratic rule even before the end of World War I. There was much happening in Europe at that time. The prevailing ideologies of socialism, Marxism, nationalism, racism, and autocracy divided the people into various camps and gave rise to a number of major movements. Communism and fascism had been in competition with each other for some time. Nazism came into the picture somewhat later. To make sure they succeeded, all three of these movements resorted to propaganda, telling the various ideological groups what they wanted to hear. In most cases, these movements approached their campaigns with a mixture of selected elements from the various ideologies. As Davies pointed out, for example, "communism and fascism were radical movements which developed ideologies professing a blend of nationalist and socialist elements."[3]

Because of the social and economic problems of that time, people questioned the viability of democracy and looked for a different system to improve their lives. Dictators and potential dictators took advantage of the situation and tried to appeal to the masses with all kinds of utopian visions. While the visions these dictators projected varied, they all "cherished," according to Davies, "the vision of a New Man who was to create a New Order cleansed of all present impurities."[4]

As a result of the just described ferment in Europe, Benito Mussolini succeeded in becoming the dictator of Italy in 1922.

Adolph Hitler took over Germany in 1933 and quickly absorbed other countries located around Germany. The Bolsheviks had already established their order in Russia in 1917 and moved toward the creation of the Soviet Union by imposing their rule in the Russian periphery. Military coups took place in Portugal, Greece, Spain, and in several other countries in South America. Yugoslavia and Bulgaria became more autocratic than they were initially. Meanwhile, Albania's six-month trial with democracy in 1924 fell victim to a warlord from Northern Albania who took over the country by force and, four years later, declared himself king. He ruled the country until 1939 when Mussolini invaded the country and made it a part of what he considered to be his Italian empire. As Huntington concluded, "[T]he war that had been fought to make the world safe for democracy had instead unleashed movements of both the Right and the Left that were intent on destroying it."[5]

The second wave of democracy coincided with World War II. It was a short wave stretching from the early 1940s to the early 1960s. The countries included in this wave were mainly the defeated countries of Italy and Japan and the part of Germany that came to be known at that time as West Germany. Also included were some of those countries Italy, Japan, and Germany had occupied, such as Austria, Czechoslovakia, Hungary, France, Belgium, and the Netherlands. Following her liberation from the Nazis, Greece was also able to regain her democratic rule and survived as a democracy despite a long and bitter civil war between the government forces and those forces supported by the communist movement. In the Far East, Japan was made democratic, while Korea gained her freedom from Japan and eventually adopted democratic institutions. A good number of South American countries moved toward democracy, as well. In addition, the end of colonial rule enabled a significant number of countries, especially in Asia and Africa, to join the democratic movement.

As had happened with the first wave of democracy, the second wave also suffered reverses. The cold war and military coups were the main causes for many countries reverting to authoritarian rule. Eastern European countries that were liberated by the Soviet Union, some of them with prior democratic tradition, "were finding," as Davis points out, "that their liberation was joined to a new form of subjugation."[6] The Soviet Union was all along claiming to be a democracy, but their system was a democracy only in structure. Though they referred to themselves as a people's democracy, the Soviets' emphasis was entirely on the state and the supremacy of the Communist Party. Freedom and other rights were totally ignored. As Mastellone concluded, "[T]he monocratic Soviet one-party system was, in reality, the antithesis of democracy."[7] The countries under Soviet influence included Poland, Czechoslovakia, Hungary, Romania, Bulgaria, the Baltic States, the region known then as Yugoslavia, and what came to be known after the war as East Germany.

Most of the countries reverting to autocracy, however, were the result of military coups. They happened throughout the world, especially in South America, Asia, and Africa. Included among them were large countries such as Argentina, Brazil, Chile, Indonesia, the Philippines, and Nigeria. Greece, the only democratic nation in Albania's neighborhood, also fell to a military coup in 1967. According to an estimate provided by Huntington, "one-third of 32 working democracies in the world in 1958 had become authoritarian by the mid-1970s."[8] Once again, despite much hope and anticipation, another world war did not make the world safe for democracy.

Following the end of the Nazi occupation in 1944, Albania was taken over by the communist underground under the leadership of Enver Hoxha. This man ruled the country with an iron fist until his death in 1985. He was replaced by Ramiz Alia who continued ruling autocratically.

Of all three of the waves of democracy, the third one was the most impressive. Beginning with Portugal and Greece in 1974, democracies emerged in just about every part of the world. Dictators fell in South America and were replaced by elected governments. In Asia, several countries returned to democratic rule, including India, Pakistan, and the Philippines. As a continuing result of colonialism's fall during the second wave, more democratic countries emerged in various parts of the world, including Africa. Authoritarian states did survive but many of them attempted various degrees of liberalization. The most dramatic development was the fall of communism that allowed several European countries to regain democratic rule. A number of former Soviet republics gained their independence while others experimented with various levels of democratic governance. The people of Albania, especially the youth, joined the anticommunist movement and forced a degree of liberalization in Alia's harsh rule. This led eventually to multiparty elections.

The third wave was greeted with great enthusiasm, and hopes for the future of democracy were very high. Commenting about the third-wave successes, Huntington wrote in 1991 that "the movement toward democracy seemed to take on the character of an almost irresistible global tide moving on from one triumph to the next."[9] As a result, the percentage of all countries that turned democratic worldwide increased from 27.5 percent in 1974 to 46 percent in 1990 to 61 percent in 1996. Between 1989 and 1996 the number of electoral democracies in the world increased from 76 to 118.[10]

It is probably too early at this point to talk about reverses in the third wave of democracy, but a number of countries, mainly former republics of the Soviet Union, were reluctant to join the movement. Some argued for postponement of democratization until the proper conditions were developed to support democracy. Others, including Russia, briefly tried democracy but were overwhelmed by the challenges it presented. As a result, they reverted to authoritarian practices and limited freedoms.

Questioning Existing Democratization Models and Searching for a New One

Elated by the overwhelming turn toward democracy, well-established democracies, especially the United States and the European Union countries, rushed with experts and resources to assist with democracy building. At the same time, scholars tried to identify the basic conditions of democracy and the process to best develop these conditions. Juan J. Lintz and Alfred Stepan argued that a democracy cannot function properly without the following conditions: a functioning state, a strong civil society consisting of individuals who take seriously their role as citizens, a formal political society functioning on the basis of established rules and procedures, a legal system that is highly respected by all, a state bureaucracy that is guided by the common good and abides by a set of laws, and a healthy economic society. The authors believe, in addition, that the people in a consolidated democracy must develop habitual behaviors and attitudes that are opposed to antidemocratic forces and support democratic principles and practices. Furthermore, they are convinced that "a democratic regime is consolidated when governmental and nongovernmental forces alike become subject to, and habituated to, the resolution of conflict within the bounds of the specific laws, procedures, and institutions sanctioned by the new democratic process."[11]

But what is the best way to develop these conditions? There was no model available for those scholars and practitioners working in countries that needed assistance to move from authoritarian rule to democracy. Eventually, they arrived at a process that came to be known as the *transition paradigm*, which was the first democratization model. Simply described, it consists of three basic steps: opening, breakthrough, and consolidation. A variety of events and circumstances lead the people of a country under authoritarian rule to an opening—a relaxation of the rules. A breakthrough then emerges, such as the formation of political parties or scheduling of free elections. These two steps can be taken within a short period, but consolidation is a rather lengthy and difficult process. It requires free and fair elections and the adoption of liberal policies and practices that should forever continue to improve and advance to higher levels. Andreas Schedler presents the democratization process in the form of subcategories of democracy, advancing from authoritarian rule to electoral democracy, to liberal democracy and, finally, to advanced democracy. The majority of democracies, including those in transition, find themselves in the middle two subcategories: the electoral, trying to survive by avoiding setbacks, and the liberal, trying to make progress toward further consolidation.[12] As Guillermo O'Donnell wrote, democracy always "looks toward a better future, expected and demanded by human beings who recognize themselves as carriers of inalienable rights that the political realm should respect and foster."[13]

How successful was the transition paradigm? Serious concerns were expressed about the effectiveness of democratization as early as 1996. "There are indications," Huntington wrote during that year, "that a new reverse wave may be gathering which could lead to the erosion of some third wave gains."[14] In 2002, Thomas Carothers went as far as to publish an article in the *Journal of Democracy* (January 2002) under the title, "The End of the Transition Paradigm." The article questioned the assumptions of the paradigm and concluded that it is time "to recognize that the transition paradigm has outlived its usefulness and to look for a better lens."[15]

In January 2007, Carothers published another article with which he again challenged the effectiveness of the transition paradigm. He argued in this article that the inability of the transition paradigm to adequately advance democracy rests on the neglect of prior conditions. He reminded us that promoters of democracy were too quick to assume that, by following the steps of the transition paradigm, democracy could be built anywhere and by anyone. "In so doing," he wrote, "they tended to underestimate the complications that different underlying conditions could present and to overestimate the power of elections alone to produce fundamental political change."[16]

In view of the continuing challenges to the transition paradigm, several other models developed. Some countries, including some former republics of the Soviet Union, did turn their attention toward the *Asian authoritarianism model* for building their democracy. This model calls for the development of a rigorous capitalist market economy, under the guidance of a strong authoritarian regime, before any attempt can be made to elect a democratic government. Malaysia and South Korea are considered good examples of this model. China's successes with market economy made the model even more attractive.[17]

Another approach, known as the *sequencing model*, is similar to the Asian authoritarian model, but calls for the postponement of democratization until certain specific conditions are met. Edward D. Mansfield and Jack Snyder advocated this model for countries such as those which emerged from the dissolution of former Yugoslavia. Observing that a fast track toward the democratization of these countries ran into serious internal conflicts and wars with neighbors, they recommended postponing democratization until the rule of law and a well-functioning state are first in place.[18]

As he did with the transition paradigm, Carothers also rejected the sequencing model with another article entitled "The 'Sequencing' Fallacy." He argued that postponing democracy development until the rule of law and a well-functioning state are in place is really an excuse on the part of authoritarian rulers to continue their grip in power. Carothers concludes that "the idea of sequencing is problematic, as are the policy recommendations that flow from it."[19]

Mansfield and Snyder immediately published a response to Carothers article defending their positions. They argued that "it is dangerous to push states to democratize before the necessary preconditions are in place and that prudent democracy-promotion efforts should pay special attention to fostering those preconditions."[20] Francis Fukuyama joined the debate with a public response in which he stated that he was "broadly sympathetic" to Carothers's arguments. At the same time, he found "nothing wrong in principle" with sequencing, but pointed out "that the number of cases where one can find genuine development-minded autocrats is extremely small."[21] Finally, Sheri Berman responded by pointing out that there are two types of preconditionists (as she referred to them)—the old and the new. The old preconditionists argue that one should wait for preconditions to be established before attempting to democratize the government and politics, while the new preconditionists want to deal with existing preconditions as soon as any attempt at democratization is undertaken.[22] Berman tends to lean more toward the Carothers position.

It appears from the discussion that instead of the transition paradigm and the sequencing model, Carothers prefers an approach that he refers to as *gradualism*. Instead of postponing democracy building until preconditions are in place, democratization should start right away. It should deal with the political aspects of democracy and the significant underlying conditions of society at the same time. The underlying conditions Carothers identifies are as follows: level of economic development, concentration of resources of national wealth, identity-based divisions, historical experience with political pluralism, and nondemocratic neighborhoods. These conditions derived from observations that democratization moves forward more effectively in situations where the economy is healthy, national wealth comes from a variety of sources, the country has some past experience with political pluralism, multiple identities are accepted and respected, and the neighboring countries are mostly democratic.[23]

While remaining faithful to his gradualism model, Carothers ignored all totalitarian models and suggested two basic approaches to democratization in a recent article —the *political approach* and the *developmental approach*. The first is narrower and its concerns are elections and political liberties. The second has a broader base and "encompasses concerns about equality and justice and the concept of democratization as a slow iterative process of change involving an interrelated set of political and socioeconomic developments."[24] Though the details may vary from one situation to the other, effective democratization requires dealing with both political aspects and societal conditions at the same time. As revealed by the debate and my experiences, this appears to be the consensus.

Placing the Albanian Experiment within the Democratization Debate

Where does Albania's democracy-building experiment fit within the overall democratization debate? As already mentioned, Albania turned away from authoritarianism during the third wave of democracy. As elaborated in chapter 1, the switch was motivated by Gorbachev's glasnost policies and the revolutions that followed in the various nations controlled by the communists. As the reader may recall, Alia and his supporters tried to dismiss what was happening in Eastern Europe by blaming revisionists for glasnost, and local hooligans for the various unrests. However, Alia and company no longer had the people's trust and the pressure for change continued. Using a term from the transition paradigm, the *opening* toward democracy emerged in Shkodra with the death of a student during a demonstration. As Eliz Biberj confirms, more reforms followed,[25] but the people, especially the students, were demanding drastic changes, including the formation of multiple political parties and free elections. At the same time, the military demonstrated a reluctance to intervene.

Overtaken by this atmosphere, Alia organized a committee to meet with students and try to convince them not to resort to extremes. One of the members of this committee was Dr. Sali Berisha, a cardiologist and a member of the communist elite. While working with the students, he emerged as the leader of the opposition and eventually organized the Democratic Party. Forced by the circumstances, the Albanian Party of Labor, the only political party in existence, agreed to the establishment of the Democratic Party under the leadership of a trusted, as they thought, member of the communist leadership. This led to the formation of additional parties, a development that in the framework of the transition paradigm can be considered to be the *breakthrough* step in the democratization process of Albania. At this point of the events, Berisha openly urged the intellectuals toward openness and a free debate on the nature of the Albanian society.

On March 31, 1991, the Democratic Party, under Berisha's leadership, participated in the elections as the main opposition party to the Albanian Party of Labor. In view of the continuing unrests, the communists campaigned as the law and order party and used all kinds of mechanisms to confuse the people on the issues and keep the opposition from campaigning widely. The Albanian Party of Labor won the elections, mainly with the support of the people in the countryside who were concerned about security, given the progressing unrest. The economy was in shambles and the best hope for any Albanian was to find a way to leave the country. In the midst of all this, the government did not survive. Another election took place in March 1992 under the eye of international observers. The Democratic Party won this election, and Berisha became the president of the Republic. In the vocabulary of the transition paradigm, a new *electoral democracy* was established.[26]

The international community was elated with the outcome, but in the long run politics and the situation in general did not evolve as well as expected. In the judgment of the international observers, the legitimacy of the next elections, four years later, was widely questioned. A few months later, the economy collapsed due to the failure of a pyramid scheme in which the people lost their savings. This situation, plus the dissatisfaction with the elections, caused a revolution in 1997 that could not be contained. International forces were invited in the country to establish order and organize new elections. The Democratic Party was defeated and the former Albanian Party of Labor won under the new name of Socialist Party. The socialists were reelected four years later, but after they finished a second term, they were voted out of office in 2005 and Berisha's Democratic Party returned to power with him as prime minister, due to a change in the system of government in which the president of the country has very limited powers.

While all this was happening in the political realm, and as early as 1992, the UW project came into being in Albania to advocate the development of democracy from within. As already elaborated, the intention of the project's leadership was to start at the local level and approach democratization from the bottom up. Furthermore, the project was probably the only one of its kind using the educational system, including the universities, as the basic conduit for the democratization of the entire country. If democracy was to be consolidated in Albania, the impetus had to come from the people at the local level, especially the younger generation which was growing up without the influences of communist propaganda. As one of the Albanian vice ministers of education once remarked, "The hope for a democratic Albania rests with the children of the country. Unfortunately, adults grew up under a harsh Communist regime and were inflicted by the disease of authoritarian communism, which cannot be cured."[27]

The UW project put the democratization process in Albania in two paths. On the one hand, the political leaders worked to develop political parties and institutions of the government. Also, the political leaders organized and carried out elections. This is typical of what happens in countries that follow the transition paradigm. The UW project on the other hand, used a developmental approach through education to empower individuals to improve their living conditions and participate in the democratization process. People were learning how to think and develop skills useful in everyday life. For instance, teachers, and the young people entrusted to them, were instructed on how to engage in dialogue, resolve conflicts through compromise, and temper self-interest while giving more attention to the common good. They were also instructed on understanding their relationship with their government within the context of rights and responsibilities. All these are crucial for the development of democracy.

One may conclude that the UW project's approach brings it closer to Carothers' gradualism model, dealing with politics and development at the same time. In reality, however, the overall democratization process in Albania was quite unique. While the political aspects of democracy were in the government's hands, the project addressed some of the underlying conditions separately during the same time. This does not mean that the project totally ignored the political aspects of democracy or that the project had no connection with the political and governmental authorities. The project needed the approval of the government and several politicians participated in various project activities at the local level. National conferences were also organized and brought together government officials, politicians, and educators to discuss matters related to the democratization process. But it can still be argued that the overall approach to democratization in Albania during the 1990s and the first few years of the new century was closer to Carothers approach—addressing underlying conditions in society, while the government was developing the political aspects of democracy.

What lies ahead for the future of Albania as far as democratization is concerned? Regardless of the continuing problems within the political realm and the limited scope of the UW project, progress toward democratization is evident in Albania. A very encouraging element is the fact that the overwhelming majority of the Albanian people continue to demonstrate a feeling that democracy is the best option for them. It is my strong conviction that, sooner or later, Albania will be classified as a free country and thus become a member of the European Union. I should emphasize, however, that it can be sooner, rather than later, provided the Albanian Government and the European Union adopt the proposal presented in the next and final chapter of this book.

10

Presenting a New Model for Albania and Beyond

Assessing the Current Status of Democratization in Albania

The proposal presented in this chapter can be applied anywhere and especially in those countries that emerged from the dissolution of the former Soviet Union. It should be emphasized, however, that the proposal evolved from within the context of the democratization effort in Albania. Consequently, it reflects the conditions in that country and the current dynamics as they are shaped by the various relevant players at the scene. It is appropriate, therefore, to start this chapter with an assessment of democracy in Albania and an analysis of the current status of democratization in that country. The effectiveness, as well as the adequacy, of the current and past players will also be examined.

One of the most recognized information sources for the assessment of democracy around the world is Freedom House, a United States-based nonprofit organization with representatives and researchers in every country. Using surveys, they collect data on political rights and civil liberties from every country. The political rights consist of the following areas: electoral process, political pluralism and participation, and functioning government. The civil liberties are freedom of expression and belief, associational and organizational rights, rule of law, and personal autonomy and individual rights. Following the collection and treatment of data, Freedom House rates each country on a seven-point scale from 1 (representing the most-free country) to 7 (representing the most-totalitarian country). Those countries falling in the range of 1.0–2.5 are classified as *Free*; those in the range of 3.0–5.0 are *Partly Free*; and those in the range of 5.5–7.0 are classified as

Not Free. The findings are published annually in a volume entitled *Freedom in the World*. In the 2009 report, Albania was rated with a score of 3 in both categories of criteria—political rights and civil liberties.[1]

Considering that Albania emerged from one of the harshest dictatorial regimes, a score of 3 in political rights and civil liberties is very encouraging. However, Albania has been rated at that level since 2003—with no progress during the last several years. Why this stalemate? To find the answer, it is advisable to turn to *Nations in Transit*, another publication by Freedom House. This publication reports specifically on the twenty-nine countries, including Albania, which emerged from the area that was under the influence of the former Soviet Union. The assessment criteria for these countries have been modified to better reflect the conditions and problems these countries face. The criteria are electoral process, civil society, independent media, national democratic governance, local democratic governance, judicial framework and independence, and corruption. Following are the scores and brief comments on Albania in each one of these criteria as provided mainly by the 2008 *Nations in Transit* full report.[2] The 2009 scores on Albania are also provided by the 2009 edition of *Nations in Transit*.[3]

It is interesting to observe that in the criterion of *electoral process* Albania moved backward from a score of 3.50 in 2006 to a score of 4.0 during the years 2007 and 2008. This was due to questionable practices in elections and the inability of the political parties to agree on a new electoral system. An agreement was finally reached and the 2009 score improved to 3.75. On the criterion of *civil society*, Albania continues to be rated with a score of 3.0 since 2006. No ground was lost, but no progress was made either in advancing civil society during the last three years. It is encouraging, nevertheless, to see the score on civil society approaching the range of free countries. The various NGOs have been very active promoting democratic legislation, even though they operate with limited resources. "Civil society organizations," the 2008 report states, "still lack sustainable resources, organizational capacities, and advocacy skills."[4] However, as reported in the 2009 report, the situation did not improve.[5]

Another critical sector for democratic development that faces problems in Albania is the *public media*. Its independence continues to be threatened. Freedom House rated the public media with a score of 3.75 in 2006, 2007, 2008, and 2009. No progress was made since 2006. There are plenty of newspapers, television stations, and radio stations, but their mission is primarily to serve the interests of the government or those of their owners. At the same time, the government demonstrates a lack of ability, or maybe willingness, to safeguard the independence of the media. What happens in Albania with the media is similar to what Professor Farkas tells us is happening throughout most of Southeast Europe. "Politicians still seem prone," he points out, "to see media as an asset for the opposition and a liability for the regime—despite the many cases of regime manipulation of the media."[6]

In 2005, Freedom House split the criterion of governance into two criteria for the 29 nations in transit. The two new criteria are national democratic governance and local democratic governance. *National democratic governance* moved backward from a score of 4.0 in 2006 to a score of 4.25 in 2007, 2008, and 2009. The critical problem with national democratic governance is mainly a demonstrated lack of respect on the part of the Executive Branch for the independence of the Judiciary and other independent institutions. Unfortunately, the opposition was unable to do anything about the situation due to lack of unity. As concluded in *Nations in Transit 2008*, "[O]n the whole, national democratic governance in Albania in 2007 was characterized by the ruling coalition's tendency to control independent institutions . . . through the appointment of figures closely linked with the ruling coalition, and the failure of a splintered opposition to capitalize on this trend."[7] The 2009 executive summary reports similar problems. For example, "[T]he ruling party continues," the report says, "to demonstrate its tendency to control the judiciary rather than propose an all-inclusive strategy on how to reform the justice system."[8]

On the other hand, *local democratic governance* was rated since 2006 with a score of 2.75—the best thus far for Albania. Local governance was strengthened recently through the influence of the European Union (EU). Local governments were established throughout Albania in the form of 65 municipalities in the urban areas and 308 communes in the rural areas. A number of powers were transferred from the national government to the local governments. This was not done, of course, without tensions between the two levels. For example, a law passed unanimously in 2008 to enable loans to local governments for long-term investments at the local level; as the 2009 report points out, "the Ministry of Finance has yet to complete the subordinate legal acts for implementing this law."[9]

The last two criteria used by Freedom House to assess democracy in the 29 countries are judicial framework and independence and corruption. As far as the *judicial framework and independence* is concerned, the sector improved somewhat from a score of 4.25 in 2006 to a score of 4.0 in 2007 and 2008. Unfortunately, the score went back to 4.25 in 2009. "The judiciary continues to be perceived," says the report, "as one of the most corrupt segments of the society."[10] This is, most likely, the main reason for which Albania received in 2007, 2008, and 2009 a score of 5.0 in corruption—the lowest in value at this point of all scores. In the 2008 *Corruption Perceptions Index* report, issued by Transparency International, Albania was ranked 85th out of 180 countries surveyed.[11] The 2009 executive summary on nations in transit reports that "[O]ne of the most dramatic failures of the government and its 'clean hands' policy can be measured by the way it has handled corruption within its own ranks. Two key ministers from the cabinet faced criminal proceedings for corruption scandals in 2008."[12]

The best case scenario is that the information in the preceding paragraphs contains mixed developments. One may conclude that the Freedom House reports reveal an overall improvement in the development of a civil society in Albania. It also points to significant progress in the development of a well-functioning system of governance at the local level. Though some disturbing practices are still evident in the electoral process, multiparty participation in elections is a reality, and the transfer of power takes place in a rather peaceful manner. However, there is a dire need for more attention to be directed toward improving the areas of national governance and corruption. The government needs to demonstrate more respect for the independence of the judiciary and the public media. Politicians in general need to commit themselves to the common good as the people define it, avoid polarization, and deal with each other civilly.

Using the Freedom House scale of 1–7, Albania is rated in the 2009 *Nations in Transit* report with an overall score of 3.82. This places the country within the range of 3.0–5.0 and classifies it as a partly free country. Considering that in 2002 Albania was rated with an overall score of 4.75, progress has been made, but there is still work to be done before moving into the range of free counties, which is 1.0–2.5.

Assessing the Impact of the EU's Consideration of Albania for Admission

One indication that Albania made good progress toward democratization is the fact that the EU officially decided in 2005 to consider Albania for admission to that promising group of countries. Since one of the criteria for admission is the development of democratic institutions, the assessment of democratization in Albania will not be complete without considering Albania's progress toward that objective, as viewed by the EU specialists. How is the EU determining progress toward democratization? What criteria do they use for the assessment and how comparable these criteria are with those used by Freedom House? Are there any criteria the EU is applying more prominently than Freedom House does? Finally, is the EU aware of the University of Washington (UW) project in Albania and the impact it had on the democratization of the country?

To respond to these questions, I pursued a grant from the EU and on June 17, 2008, visited its headquarters in Brussels, Belgium. In preparation for the trip, I sent a letter to the Albanian Desk asking for an appointment. I also stated my purpose in the form of a few questions similar to those in the previous paragraph. The time for the requested appointment was approaching and I had no response. The appointment finally arrived and I flew to Brussels as previously scheduled. A day later, I met with the appropriate officials and soon realized why my appointment notification was so late. My letter had been circulated in various parts of Europe, and they were waiting for responses to my questions. One such response came from Turin, Italy, written by Margarita Nikolovska who is involved with Vocational Education in Albania. She wrote that the project "had a big impact on improvements in the curricula, and therefore it made significant impact on democratization of education in the country."[13]

My discussion with the officials revealed that the EU is applying a topdown approach to the democratization of Albania. Most often, the EU works directly with the Albanian Government. In contrast, our project used the bottom-up approach, working through the educational system. As the discussion continued, however, we agreed that it takes both approaches to achieve consolidation of democracy in a particular country. As far as the criteria used for assessing progress in democratization, the officials were kind enough to supply me with the relevant annual reports issued since 2005. I was aware, of course, that the Commission of the EU had decided in 2004 to form a European Partnership with Albania for admission purposes. Following that agreement, a delegation of the EU was established in Tirana to assist Albania toward meeting the criteria for admission.

A careful review of the EU criteria, as outlined in the 2008 report, reveals that its criteria are much broader than those of Freedom House. While the latter is limited to political rights, and civil liberties, the EU goes further and deals, as well, with detailed economic criteria and an array of standards having to do with internal operational matters of the EU. It is clear, however, that those criteria labeled as *political* are very similar to those in the two Freedom House categories of political rights and civil liberties. The seven Freedom House criteria in the two categories just mentioned were listed earlier in chapter 9. The parallel EU criteria—those labeled political, fall into three subcategories: democracy and the rule of law, human rights and respect for and protection of minorities, and regional issues and international obligations.[14]

The first subcategory, democracy and the rule of law, focuses on the following areas: *parliament, government, public administration, judicial system*, and *anticorruption policy*. All of these areas are also included in the list of the Freedom House criteria. The second subcategory—human rights and respect and protection of minorities—includes *observance of international human rights law; civil and political rights; economic and social rights; and minority rights, cultural rights, and protection of minorities*. Compared to Freedom House, it appears that the EU pays more attention to economic rights and minority rights. The regional issues and international obligations category concerns regional cooperation and bilateral relations with other members or prospective members of the EU. These criteria are unique to the EU.

What is the assessment of the EU professionals regarding progress toward democratization in Albania? Based on information provided by the 2008 report of the Commission of the European Communities, some progress was acknowledged in all areas related to the various criteria. At the same time, however, all positive comments are followed by the identification of critical problems needing urgent attention, especially in the area of implementation of related legislation. In the criterion of *democracy and the rule of law*, the two largest political parties started cooperating with each other on important legislation "relating to the electoral system, election of the President and the mandate of the Prosecutor General."[15] The government also developed policies with which to guide integration with the EU. "The existing requirements, however, for public consultation on EU-related policy work, under the government rules of procedure, are not fully applied."[16] Public Administration "is continuing to stabilize, but the lack of transparency and accountability in appointments is endangering its independence."[17] The areas in which Albania has serious problems are the judicial system and corruption. According to the 2008 EU report, "the justice system continues to function poorly due to shortcomings in independence, accountability and transparency."[18] When it comes to corruption, a strong commitment was declared recently to fight it, but as the same report concludes, that commitment "needs to be backed up by rigorous implementation, as corruption remains widespread."[19]

Turning to human rights and the protection of minorities, the 2008 report reminds us that Albania has not yet ratified the European Charter for Regional and Minority Languages. On the other hand, it is reported that "the Human Rights Ombudsman has contributed to reducing human rights violations."[20] Some efforts were made "to prevent torture and ill-treatment of detainees, but considerably better enforcement of human rights rules and proper prosecution of abusers are required."[21] It is also reported that "detention standards remain very poor."[22] Turning to freedom of expression and freedom of the press, they are guaranteed in Albania and continue to improve, but the need is there "to improve implementation of the existing legislation and to advance on key issues regarding decriminalization of defamation, adoption of legislation on access to public information and transparency of media ownership."[23]

There is indeed a legal framework in Albania for freedom of assembly and association. The EU 2008 report points out, however, that "[C]ivil society should increase its capacity for advocacy and public relations, networking, and development of partnerships with the government and private sector."[24] Freedom of religion and the way the various faiths relate with each other are commendable in Albania. "However, the full restitution of properties and other belongings to religious communities remains an issue to be addressed as part of the overall property restitution efforts."[25] Room is also available for the improvement of the rights of women, children, the disabled, and labor.

Compared to the Freedom House report, property rights and minority rights are more prominently emphasized in the EU report. As the reader may recall, all land in Albania had been confiscated by the communist regime and was used for a variety of public purposes. When the regime fell, people claimed for private purposes pieces of land that were either public or private before the takeover by the communists. At the same time, the rightful owners before the regime were demanding their property. This created a mess and a way had to be found to resolve the situation. In most cases, prior owners were allowed to either reclaim their property or be compensated for it. Some illegal buildings were destroyed to make the property available for the original owners. There are still tens of thousands of claims for restitution to be considered by the recently established Property Restitution and Compensation Agency (PRCA). A list of claims and their valuation is now prepared. "A completed valuation map covering every region," the 2008 report argues, "would facilitate assessment of property restitution and compensation issues."[26]

Also, as far as the EU is concerned, the establishment of minority rights is a crucial step toward the democratization of Albania. There are several ethnic minority groups in the country with a history of discomfort and discrimination throughout the years, especially during the communist era. As the EU report confirms, "Albania has no accurate data on minorities."[27] Whatever their count is, they are now free in many ways, but some past undemocratic practices still linger on making the minority people wonder about their future. Schools in minority areas are not sufficient in the language of the minority, especially at the secondary level. As the 2008 report points out, "more efforts are needed on defusing recent intra-ethnic tensions in areas with a heavy concentration of minorities."[28] Also urged is "the collection of sound data on all minorities."[29] It appears that a stronger commitment is needed for the protection of minority rights. The government should see to it that the treatment of minorities improves to the point where the country will agree to sign the European Charter for Regional and Minority Languages.

Following the completion of the manuscript for this book, the EU issued the 2009 progress report on Albania.[30] The pattern followed in this report is similar to the one issued for 2008. Some progress is recognized in certain areas, but much remains to be done, especially in national governance, the judicial system, and corruption. The scores in the 2009 Freedom House report reveal no progress at all—they remain exactly as they were in 2008.[31]

As the EU continues to assist Albania toward admission, the people of that country continue to demonstrate a strong preference for movement in that direction. As verified by Farkas, "EU membership is the voters' highest priority. More than 80 percent report favoring prioritizing Albania's EU membership."[32] Why is the government taking so long to effectively respond to the wishes of the people? As the EU reports demonstrate year after year, what needs to be done is very clear, but that might not be the basic problem. Recent democratization literature points to the possibility that the problem may be lying deeper than just lack of awareness of what needs to be done. It may be lying on the perpetuation by those in authority of what Welzel and Inglehart referred to as "deep-rooted orientations or strong motivations."[33] Shaped by a troubled past, these orientations and motivations serve as serious roadblocks to democratic development. One needs to remember that, though Albanians go far back in history, the country of Albania, as we know it, is new—less than one hundred years old. During that period, the country experienced only the frenzy of nationalism and the pressures of a fifty-year-long harsh communist dictatorship. The country did not have much of an experience with democratic rule before 1992. As pointed out elsewhere, an attempt for democracy was made in 1924, but it lasted only for a few months.

Under these circumstances, it is almost natural for one to assume that all Albanian adults, including their leaders, carry with them "deep-rooted orientations or strong motivations" that are antithetical to the democratic way of life. Such orientations and motivations tend to be more powerful at times than the expressed overall desire on the part of the Albanian population to democratize their country. It is fair to say, however, that the conditions in Albania, or in any of the other Balkan countries, are what they are, not necessarily because those in power want them to be that way, but because they cannot help it. For example, it is their orientation from the past that compels government leaders to dictate to the people rather than seek advice from them. That was the way it was done for as long as they remember. Using their position for personal gain is too often viewed by public administrators not as corruption, but as the only way for them to survive. That was how people were surviving for decades during the times the government was controlling all resources. During the era of nationalism, it was a matter of patriotism to use any means to assimilate the various minorities within a country. Treating minorities with respect is a relatively new concept in the Balkan region.

Careful analysis of the various shortfalls in the democratization process of Albania easily convinces one that they are the result of old orientations and motivations. As a result, it may be that the country's consolidation of democracy will not materialize until the younger generation takes over. Hopefully, people of that generation will be free of past orientations and motivations. As such, they will be in a better position to be guided in their actions by the future and the common good of the entire society. However, waiting for that to happen would be a defeatist strategy. It makes no sense for Albania to wait that long when the door of the EU is open for them to enter. Why lose this opportunity?

While I was still in Europe, I was determined to find a way that could drive democratization in Albania forward more quickly. But first, I had to return to Albania to explore the current situation. So I flew from Brussels to Tirana for a few days to witness the current dynamics and get a feeling of the current direction the various players were taking the country. I also wanted to discuss with as many as possible of my coworkers in Albania the future of democratization in that country, and beyond. The leadership team of the UW project was anxiously waiting for me with a full and thoughtfully prepared schedule and agenda.

RESTRUCTURING THE PROCESS FOR FASTER DEMOCRATIZATION IN ALBANIA

After meeting with officials of the EU Delegation in Tirana, I met with the minister of integration, Dr. Majlinda Bregu, a very impressive and forward looking young woman. We briefly discussed the progress made thus far toward meeting the admissions criteria of the EU. In addition, I met with the members of the Standing Parliamentary Committee on European Integration. I also spent as much time as I could with the UW project leaders, Drs. Marjana Sinani and Milika Dhamo. It soon became clear to me that all Albanians appreciated the involvement of the EU, but they found their requests for change to be overwhelming. Though somewhat frustrated, they were anxious to see democratization move forward at a faster pace.

It did not take me long to conclude that the EU is, at the present time, a major player in the process of democratization in Albania. As they usually do, they are working directly with the government using the topdown approach. They identify the changes to be made and constantly advise the government on how to proceed. In an effort to improve economic conditions, they also initiated certain vocational education activities. The civic education centers and the rest of the democratization network developed by the UW project continue to operate, but they are not contributing to maximum capacity due to inadequate funding that forced them to a degree of marginalization. As pointed out earlier in this chapter, the NGOs find themselves in a similar condition. They are active, but they could be more so, provided they had the kind of support they deserve.

The EU is, thus far, the only player that is pursuing its role with vigor in advising the Albanian government and advancing recommendations. But as demonstrated earlier, the data show that the government is not as effective as it needs to be in adequately responding to the recommendations. In fact, it is quite obvious from the assessment that the source of difficulty in accelerating Albanian democratization lies mainly with the government. Those in authority at any level must go beyond giving lip-service to democracy and promote the democratic way of life with actions based on sound principles. But how can this be achieved? What will eliminate unending disagreements, delays in the implementation of promising legislation, and inaction on matters that can make a difference?

The inspiration for a solution to this problem came from Welzel and Inglehart's article mentioned earlier in this chapter. They emphasize in this article that government elites alone cannot succeed in the development of a consolidated democracy. In their words, "it is insufficient to focus only on elites—increasingly, one must also study mass-level developments."[34] This recommendation is very much in line with the conclusion reached in the previous chapter. Democracy cannot be developed by the government without the active and systematic participation of the people and the improvement of the conditions that facilitate their participation.

The Welzel and Inglehart article reminded me of the successes we experienced as we were working with children and youth in the schools around Albania. They had no difficulty grasping the value of democracy and putting it into action at the local level. Whether it was helping those in need, developing plans to clean their environment, or just discussing issues in a civil and orderly manner, they were succeeding and exhibiting a sense of satisfaction and pride. Their parents and invited local officials were pleased to join the activities. They were just as excited and proud as the students were with the opportunity to be a part of what they perceived to be meaningful contributions to their community. These memories convinced me that Albanian democracy would be better served if this kind of spirit could become a reality for all ordinary citizens.

With the above thoughts in mind, the solution to the problems faced by democratization in Albania was obvious. *The ordinary citizens had to be mobilized to play an active role in the democratization of the country.* What we did with the children and youth in the schools should also be done with the adults. Such a movement would be consistent with the principle of "democracy from within," and it would generate a significantly modified approach to democratization. *With the addition of the ordinary citizens, instead of two partners working together—the government and outside assistance—there would be three partners.* With this approach, the ordinary citizens will become advocates for the democratic ways and will serve as mediators between the government and the EU. The EU can advise the government but they cannot compel it to act. *In a democratic system, the ordinary citizens are the most appropriate agents to pressure the government.* When the people are involved, society is geared toward the collective benefit. Without the involvement of the people, the majority of them face difficulties, while the few take advantage of the opportunity to benefit personally.

This approach—where the ordinary citizens play a critical role in the democratization process—can be considered a new democratization model. To be successful, however, the structure and conditions of this model should be as follows:

1. The structure should consist of the following three partners:

    - Outside assistance (the EU in Albania)
    - The government
    - The ordinary citizens

2. The partnership should operate under the following conditions:

    - All three partners are of equal importance,
    - The roles and limitations of each partner are clearly defined by legislation,
    - All government officials should participate in a limited number of seminars on democracy,
    - All ordinary citizens must be empowered for their role through intensive education focused on democracy, and
    - More attention should be given to the developmental aspects of society.

From an operational point of view, the EU and the Albanian government will continue what they are currently doing. The EU will continue identifying areas for change, setting and prioritizing annual goals for the government, and assessing progress toward the achievement of these goals. The government will concentrate on securing legislation authorizing the recommended changes. More importantly, the government will have the responsibility to make sure that authorized legislation is promptly implemented. The role of the ordinary citizens will be to monitor and, when necessary, pressure government officials to do what is required of them—facilitate legislation for changes and implement what is being legislated. It is emphasized again that the EU representatives can advise on changes, but they cannot impose them. That is the responsibility of the ordinary citizens. Welzel and Inglehart endorse this notion with the following statement: "the development of 'effective democracy' reflects the acquisition by ordinary people of resources and values that enable them effectively to pressure elites."[35]

Turning to the conditions of the new model, it is emphasized that in order for democratization to be effective, not only the ordinary citizens, but all those called upon to become democracy builders must be empowered for their role through education. In the case of the EU specialists, they have plenty of know-how and experience in what they are doing. The politicians and government officials are usually very busy. Nevertheless, they should find time to participate in a limited number of seminars conducted by well-known democracy scholars or activists. In the case of ordinary citizens, however, the training must be well organized, extensive, and continuous. This is needed especially in the Balkan countries where the people were ignored for too long. As Farkas informs us, 70 percent of the people in Southeast Europe, which includes Albania, do not believe their will is taken into consideration in the running of their respective countries. Farkas also points out that "citizens adamantly say that their only option is to participate in elections."[36] This needs to be changed.

As far as the education for the empowerment of the citizens is concerned, Albania is in an enviable position. The university-based democratic citizenship education centers established by the UW project, along with the best of the trained teachers in their region, can prepare the citizens. It will not be easy, but the centers' successful experiences with the students in the country's schools will enable them to also educate the older generation. The program will be similar to the one applied with the students, including knowledge about the concepts and principles of democracy and the acquisition of democratic skills. It will also include the development of commitment to democratic values, including what Welzel and Inglehart refer to as "self-expression values." Such values, they say, "reflect a synthesis of interpersonal trust, tolerance, and political activism that plays a crucial role in the emergence and survival of democracy."[37]

The managers of the centers and the entire membership of the UW project network have been educated on these matters and have the materials needed to conduct appropriate workshops. This book will also prove valuable as a basic manual for instruction. Needless to say, the centers will need authorization and funding. Both should come from the Ministry of Integration in cooperation with the Ministry of Education. Hopefully, the EU will recognize the potential of the citizens' role and consider assisting with funds. Drs. Sinani and Dhamo, along with the entire UW project democratization network, are the most qualified to assume the leadership of this effort. They know democracy, are committed to its principles, and have the experience in conducting workshops on a massive scale. In addition, they have experience organizing democratization activities at the local level related to the implementation of relevant pieces of legislation.

The civil-liberty-oriented NGOs will also play a role in the preparation of the ordinary citizens. They are the backbone of a civil society, and they can be significant agents within the democratization effort. As pointed out earlier, the UW project recognized their value and welcomed them to pursue their objectives through the civic education centers and the network in general. Some of them are still carrying out various projects through the centers, many of them funded by sources outside the country. The Ministry of Integration and the EU should take advantage of the zeal usually exhibited by the members of these organizations. They deserve support and encouragement to work within the context of the network, or on their own, in the preparation of ordinary citizens.

Finally, it was pointed out earlier that the EU is involved in the promotion of vocational education in Albania. This is important for the empowerment of ordinary citizens because vocational education contributes toward their economic well-being. It is difficult for ordinary citizens to participate in civic activities without economic security. As quoted by Ethan B. Kapstein and Nathan Converse, Larry Diamond recognized the importance of this notion within the context of democratization and expressed his support with following statement: "Economic inclusion is closely related to political inclusion, and thus, to democratic deepening."[38] As indicated in the preceding chapter, attention to the economic conditions of the citizens is also supported by Carothers within the context of his most recent proposals on the developmental aspects of democratization. The EU should do more to increase its role in the economic improvement of the country so that more people will be empowered to actively participate in civic activity.

In closing this section, I want to emphasize the importance of a united front for a faster movement toward the consolidation of democracy in Albania. The government and the outside assistance are critical, but they do not appear to be enough for producing the desired outcome. The current problems will continue, unless the ordinary citizens join in to play their part. This reality is embedded in another powerful statement by Welzel and Inglehart. "The essence of democracy," they say, "is that it empowers ordinary citizens. But holding elections alone will not accomplish this. It takes more than simply passing laws that formally establish political rights to empower the people; those laws must be implemented."[39]

AIMING FOR DEMOCRACY BUILDING IN ALBANIA AND BEYOND

One of the UW project's guidelines, as outlined in the first chapter, called for the project to build Albania's democracy from within through the educational system. That is why the initial activities concentrated on the preparation of Albanian educators to assume leadership roles in the project and develop all relevant instructional materials. They guided the training of the teachers on the implementation of these materials, using open and interactive teaching. As the project was moving from one stage to the next, these Albanian educators played a key role in determining the objectives and activities of each stage. The emphasis was on assisting learners to go beyond understanding democracy and develop the ability to also apply it in everyday life.

Another important guideline called for a comprehensive approach to democratization, covering the entire country. That is why all thirty-seven school districts of Albania participated in the activities of the project, thus developing a sense of ownership. Thousands of teachers and other types of educators, including university professors, were empowered as builders of democracy. Officials and ordinary people around the country were fascinated with what the students were learning. The mass media were attracted to the democratization activities, recorded them, and eventually made them available to the public.

In 2005, as the UW was ending its role of coordinating the project from outside the country, the EU started preparing Albania for admission. This was a significant development for Albania. Progress was expected and some of it is evident. Despite that, Albania is still an electoral democracy today with critical problems quite evident. Though the EU is effectively playing its role, democracy in Albania is moving too slowly toward consolidation, just as it is true in many other countries. This realization prompted me to write the book with two objectives in mind: to describe the UW project for anyone interested in replicating it; and to present the new democratization model I developed—a model that has the potential for Albania, as well as other countries, to move democracy faster toward consolidation.

It is my strong conviction that the book will be viewed by Albanians as an opportunity to contribute more decisively toward a faster consolidation of their democracy. This includes not only those Albanians currently living in their country, but also, the hundreds of thousands of them who now live and experience the benefits of democracy in other countries. I urge the EU democratization specialists and the Albanian Minister of Integration to recognize the value of my recommendations in this book and call upon all relevant actors, especially the ordinary citizens, to help achieve democratic consolidation. The evidence and the arguments presented in this book provide an opportunity for those in government, and politicians in general, to reevaluate some of their practices and focus on what will serve the good of all people in their society. Then the door will open for swift progress toward a mature democracy.

Though this book concerns mainly Albania, it also has the potential to make a difference in other countries. It is a book that goes beyond theory and demonstrates in practice what works best. It will be a useful tool in the hands of democracy builders throughout the world, at whatever stage they may be in their democratization effort. Included among these democracy builders, are all educators, at whatever level they function. Civic education teachers and social studies teachers will find the book most useful as a textbook. Democracy is a state of civilization that has to be continually nourished. It cannot be taken for granted. Democracy can easily deteriorate, if not taught formally, as well as by example.

In order for teachers to be successful as democracy builders, they have to be adequately prepared. Teacher education programs should offer at least one course on democracy for prospective teachers. Seminars on democracy should also be available for practicing teachers on a continuous basis. The book could be valuable in such courses either as a textbook or as a handy resource on the basics of democracy and democratic citizenship education. Schools and universities should seriously consider having the book available in their libraries. The same is true of public libraries.

For ordinary citizens, this book is the perfect manual to prepare them for their role in the democratization process. As elaborated earlier in this chapter, ordinary citizens have a stake in democracy and a fundamental responsibility, not only to help establish it, but also to sustain and advance it. These are not easy tasks, but this book will equip them with what they need to guide, even pressure, the government to do what is necessary to advance democracy. Ordinary citizens will learn the basic concepts and principles of democracy. In addition, they will develop commitment in the democratic values and skill on how to consider resolving issues with civility. In fact, the book was purposely written in the form of a story in order to appeal to ordinary citizens. It will help them learn as well as practice democracy.

The final admonition comes from Ted McConnell. "For self-governance to work," he wrote, "citizens must understand and actively engage in the process."[40] After all, the word "democracy" in the Greek language means "rule by the people."

Notes

Introduction

1. Marc F. Plattner, "From Liberalism to Liberal Democracy," *Journal of Democracy* (October 1999): 121.
2. John Dewey, *Democracy and Education* (New York: Macmillan, 1923), 101.
3. Barack Obama, "Text of Obama's Speech to Muslims," *Associated Press*, http://www.google.com/hostednews/ap/article/ALeqM5gkyWK7xeDw2bliPhFS6KS6KsvP.
4. Ditmir Bushati, "Albania," *Nations in Transit 2009: Democratization from Central Europe to Eurasia* (Lahman, MD: Rowman and Littlefield, 2009), 47.
5. Ibid.
6. Christian Welzel and Ronald Inglehart, "The Role of Ordinary People in Democratization," *Journal of Democracy* 19 (January 2008): 126–140.

1 The Burden of the Past and Dreaming Democracy

1. A *partisan* in Albania during World War II was a communist fighter against the Nazis and the right-leaning underground forces.
2. Stephen Hill, "Byzantium and the Emergence of Albania," in Tom Winnifrith (Ed.), *Perspectives on Albania* (London: Macmillan, 1992), 40–57; and Anton Logoreci, *The Albanians: Europe's Forgotten Survivors* (London: Victor Gollancz, 1977), 16.
3. Elez Biberaj, *Albania in Transition: The Rocky Road to Democracy* (Boulder, CO: Westview Press, 1999), 19.
4. Ibid.
5. Miranda Vickers and James Pettifer, *Albania: From Anarchy to a Balkan Identity* (New York: New York University Press, 2000), 26.
6. Biberaj, *Albania in Transition*, 36.

2 Building Relationships and Exploring Curriculum

1. Theodore Kaltsounis, "Swing toward Decision Making," *Instructor*, April 1971, 45–56.
2. Theodore Kaltsounis, "Democracy's Challenge as the Foundation of Social Studies," *Theory and Research in Social Education* (Spring 1994): 176–193.
3. 9/11 is often used in the United States to refer to September 11, 2001, the day the Twin Towers in New York City were destroyed by terrorists. Approximately three thousand people lost their lives in that event.
4. Elez Biberaj, *Albania in Transition: The Rocky Road to Democracy* (Boulder, CO: Westview Press 1999), 13.
5. The word "saranda" in Greek means "forty," as in Hagioi Saranda or Holy Forty or Saints Saranda.
6. The five millets were Muslim, Eastern or Greek Orthodox, Roman Catholic, Jewish, and Armenian. Each one of them was under the authority of their religious leader, who was directly responsible to the Sultan.
7. The title of "Patriarch" in the Eastern Orthodox Church is equivalent with the Latin title of "Pope."
8. Mark Mazower, *The Balkans: A Short History* (New York: Modern Library 2000), 39.

3 Selecting Leaders and Defining Basic Concepts

1. One of the key sources for the values was R. Freeman Butts, *The Revival of Civic Learning* (West Lafayette, IN: Phi Delta Kappa, 1980).
2. For a more detailed elaboration on the skills, refer to Theodore Kaltsounis, *Teaching Social Studies in the Elementary School: The Basics for Citizenship*, Second Edition (Englewood Cliffs, NJ: Prentice-Hall, 1987), 105–112.
3. Milika Dhamo, Tonin Gjuraj, Fatmira Myteberi, and Marjana Sinani, *Democratic Citizenship Education in Albania: A Manual for Educators* (Tirana: AEDP 1958), 46.
4. Ibid.

4 Teaching, Learning, and Teacher's Guides

1. A partisan was an underground communist fighter during World War II.

2. Skanderbeg's real name was Gjergj Kastrioti. He was a fifteenth-century warrior revered by all Albanians. He led Albanians for twenty-five years against the occupying Ottoman Turks.
3. Miranda Vickers and James Pettifer, *Albania: From Anarchy to Balkan Identity* (New York: New York University Press, 1997), 227.
4. Elez Biberaj, *Albania in Transition: The Rocky Road to Democracy* (Boulder, CO: Westview, 1999), 277.
5. Ibid., 350.
6. Ibid., 325.
7. Theodore Kaltsounis, *Curriculum Development Project for Civic Education in Albania: Final Report* (Seattle: University of Washington College of Education, 1997), 10.

5 Publishing the Materials and Starting a Network

1. Milika Dhamo, Tonin Gjuraj, Fatmira Myeberi, and Marjana Sinani, *Democratic Citizenship Education in Albania* (Tirana: UW/AEDP, 1998), 54.
2. Ibid.
3. Ibid., 56–65.
4. Ibid., 65.
5. Ibid.
6. J. N. Hook, *One Dollar Gets You Ten: TTT as an Educational Catalyst* (Durant, Oklahoma: Southeastern State College Research Foundation, 1972).
7. Theodore Kaltsounis. "A Study Concerning Third Graders' Knowledge of Social Studies Content Prior to Instruction," *Journal of Educational Research* (March 1964): 345–349.
8. S. P. McCutchen. "A Guide to Content in the Social Studies," *Social Education* (May 1956): 211–215.
9. Professor Como's letter is on file with the author.
10. Commission Staff Working Paper, *Albania: 2005 Progress Report* (Brussels: Commission of the European Communities, 2005), 20.

6 Expanding the Network and Addressing Feedback

1. The originals of the letters referred to in this chapter are on file with the author.
2. The complete messages from which the various quotations in this chapter originate are on file with the author.

7 Network Strengthening through the Universities

1. Though the terms "civic education" and "democratic citizenship education" are used interchangeably throughout this book, the title *Center for Democratic Citizenship Education* was chosen here instead of the title *Center for Civic Education*, in order to make sure a distinction is made between civic education in a democracy and civic education in a totalitarian system. In addition, the term "citizenship education" instead of "civic education" was applied to emphasize the need to teach democracy to elementary and secondary school students not only from the perspective of knowledge, but also from the perspective of practice in everyday life.
2. A Metropolitan in the Orthodox Church is the Bishop assigned to lead the affairs of the church in a particular district. It is the equivalent of the Archbishop in the Roman Catholic Church.
3. Roland Gjini, "Center for Democratic Citizenship Education," *Studenti* (December 1, 2003): 2.

8 Evaluating and Concluding the Project

1. Anthony Rebora, "Making a Difference: Carol Ann Tomlinson Explains How Differentiated Instruction Works and Why We Need It Now," *TEACHER Magazine*, September 10, 2008.
2. NWREL Center for Research, Evaluation, and Assessment, "Summative Evaluation: Measurement and Documentation of Program Impact," http://www.nwrel.org/evaluation/summative.shtml.
3. Most of the information on the summative evaluation comes from the evaluation team's report, *Evaluation of the Democratic Citizenship Education Project in Albania*, which is on file with the College of Education at the University of Washington. A copy of the report was also sent to the U.S. Department of State as an attachment to the corresponding final report.

9 Democratization and Albania's Experiment

1. Samuel P. Huntington, *The Third Wave: Democratization in the Late Twentieth Century* (Norman and London: University of Oklahoma Press, 1991), 16.
2. Salvo Mastellone, *A History of Democracy in Europe: From Montesquieu to 1989* (Florence: Centro Editoriale Toscane, 1995), 55.

3. Norman Davies, *Europe* (New York: Harper Perennial, 1996), 945.
4. Ibid.
5. Huntington , *Third Wave*, 18.
6. Davies, *Europe*, 1050.
7. Mastellone, *History of Democracy in Europe*, 262.
8. Huntington, *Third Wave*, 21.
9. Ibid.
10. Larry Diamond, "Introduction: In Search of Consolidation," in Larry Diamond, Marc F. Plattner, Yun-ha Chu, and Hung-mao Tien, *Consolidating the Third Wave Democracies* (Baltimore and London: Johns Hopkins University Press, 1997), xvi.
11. Juan J. Lintz and Alfred Stepan, "Toward Consolidated Democracies," *Journal of Democracy*, 7 (1996): 17.
12. Andreas Schedler, "What Is Democratic Consolidation?" *Journal of Democracy*, 9 (1998): 94.
13. Guillermo O'Donnell, "The Perpetual Crisis of Democracy," *Journal of Democracy*, 18 (2007): 9.
14. Samuel P. Huntington, "Democracy for the Long Haul," *Journal of Democracy*, 7 (1996): 5.
15. Thomas Carothers, "The End of the Transition Paradigm" *Journal of Democracy*, 13 (2002): 6.
16. Thomas Carothers, "The 'Sequencing' Fallacy," *Journal of Democracy*, 18 (2007): 24.
17. Huntington, "Democracy for the Long Haul," 11.
18. Edward D. Mansfield and Jack Snyder, *Electing to Fight: Why Emerging Democracies Go to War* (Cambridge, MA: MIT Press, 2005), 300 pages.
19. Ibid., 13.
20. Edward D. Mansfield and Jack Snyder, "The Sequencing 'fallacy'," *Journal of Democracy*, 18 (2007): 5.
21. Francis Fukuyama, "Liberalism versus State-building," *Journal of Democracy*, 18 (2007): 10.
22. Sheri Berman, "The Vain Hope for 'Correct' Timing," *Journal of* Democracy, 18 (2007): 14.
23. Carothers, "The 'Sequencing' Fallacy," 24.
24. Thomas Carothers, "Democracy Assistance: Political vs. Developmental?" *Journal of Democracy*, 20 (2009): 5.
25. Elez Biberaj, *Albania in Transition: The Rocky Road to Democracy* (Boulder, CO: Westview Press, 1999), 37.
26. Miranda Vickers and James Pettifer, *Albania: From Anarchy to a Balkan Identity* (New York: New York University Press, 1997), 33–54.
27. Anon, "Albania's Road to Democracy," *Research that Matters* (Seattle: UW College of Education, 2006), 9.

10 Presenting a New Model for Albania and Beyond

1. Freedom House, "Freedom in the World—Albania," http://www.freedomhouse.org/inc/content/pubs/fiw/inc_country_detail.cfm?year-2009.
2. Ditmir Bushati, "Albania: Executive Summary," *Nations in Transit 2008: Democratization from Central Europe to Eurasia* (Lanham, MD: Rowman and Littlefield, 2008), 59–75.
3. Ditmir Bushati, "Albania" *Nations in Transit 2009*: Democratization from Central Europe to Eurasia (Lanham, MD: Rowman and Littlefield, 2009), 47–63.
4. Freedom House, *Nations in Transit 2008: Democratization from Central Europe to Eurasia*, 67.
5. Bushati, "Albania," *Nations in Transit*, 2009, 49.
6. Richard P. Farkas, *Democratization in the Balkans: Prescription for a Badly Scarred Body Politic* (Boston: Northeastern University Press, 2007), 117.
7. Freedom House, *Nations in Transit 2008*, 64.
8. Bushati, "Albania," *Nations in Transit 2009*, 48.
9. Ibid., 47.
10. Ibid.
11. Anon, *Transparency International 2008 Corruption Perceptions Index*, www.transparency.org/policy_research/surveys_indices/cpi/2008.
12. Bushati, "Albania," *Nations in Transit 2009*, 50.
13. Copy of Ms. Nikolovska's message of June 17, 2008, is on file with the author.
14. Commission Staff Working Document, *Albania 2008 Progress Report* (Brussels: Commission of the European Communities, 2008), 6–18.
15. Ibid., 6.
16. Ibid., 8.
17. Ibid.
18. Ibid., 10.
19. Ibid., 11.
20. Ibid., 12.
21. Ibid.
22. Ibid.
23. Ibid., 13.
24. Ibid.
25. Ibid.
26. Ibid., 16.
27. Ibid.

28. Ibid.
29. Ibid., 17.
30. Commission Staff Working Document, *Albania 2009 Progress Report*, 6–18.
31. Bushati, "Albania," *Nations in Transit 2009*, 47.
32. Farkas, *Democratization in the Balkans*, 105.
33. Christian Welzel and Roland Inglehart, "The Role of Ordinary People in Democratization," *Journal of Democracy* 19 (January 2008): 132.
34. Ibid., 138.
35. Ibid., 126.
36. Farkas, *Democratization in the Balkans*, 116.
37. Welzel and Inglehart, "The Role of Ordinary People in Democratization," 138.
38. Ethan B. Kapstein and Nathan Converse, "Poverty, Inequality, and Democracy: Why Democracies Fail," *Journal of Democracy* (October 2008): 61.
39. Welzel and Inglehart, "The Role of Ordinary People in Democratization, 128.
40. Ted McConnell, "Not by Votes Alone...The Vital Imperative of Restoring the Civic Mission of Schools," *Social Education* (October 2008): 313.

Index

CPSIA information can be obtained
at www.ICGtesting.com
Printed in the USA
BVOW06*1314060917
494001BV00006B/67/P

9 780230 104587